HIDDEN HISTORY

of

BUCKS COUNTY

Jennifer Rogers

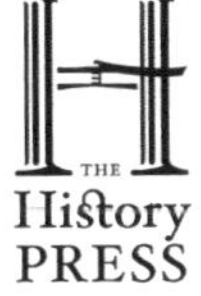

Published by The History Press
Charleston, SC
www.historypress.com

Unless otherwise noted, images are from the author's collection.

First published 2019
Updated 2024

Manufactured in the United States

ISBN 9781467138703

Library of Congress Control Number: 2018960969

Notice: The information in this book is true and complete to the best of our knowledge. It is offered without guarantee on the part of the author or The History Press. The author and The History Press disclaim all liability in connection with the use of this book.

Dedication

This book is dedicated to Dr. James Adams, a man of great wisdom, integrity and knowledge. While I was obtaining my Bachelor of Arts in American Studies at Pennsylvania State University, Dr. Adams taught six of my history courses, all the while guiding me in understanding how truly amazing history is and why it should continue to be appreciated. When Dr. Adams passed away just a year after my graduation, I, along with many of his students and colleagues, was devastated. Thank you, Dr. Adams, for making history fun, enjoyable and incredibly fascinating. I will carry your love of history with me for life.

CONTENTS

FOREWORD

Jennifer Rogers is uniquely qualified to write about the unknown aspects of Bucks County, one of Pennsylvania's most storied counties. Ms. Rogers is a skilled historic researcher who has a keen sense of what makes a fascinating story when she encounters a fragment of a diary, an enticing picture or an almost-forgotten historic inn. While she was still my student in American Studies at Penn State University's Abington College and interning at Doylestown's Mercer Museum, Rogers stumbled on an unpublished diary, handwritten in a sometimes hard-to-read faded scrawl. Intrigued, she discovered it was a firsthand account by an enlisted Civil War soldier, Private Joseph Lehman Eisenbrey, from Lumberville, Bucks County. Getting permission from the museum to transcribe the diary, Rogers spent the better part of a year following the exploits of the soldier from boot camp in Philadelphia to the end of the war at Appomattox. Captivated by his story, she extended her research into the rest of Eisenbrey's life as he became a prominent dentist in Chestnut Hill, taking photos of his former residence. Rogers's work culminated in a paper analyzing the context of Eisenbrey's part in the Civil War that was accepted for the Pennsylvania History annual conference. Rogers's persistence and skill in original research is noteworthy.

Jennifer Rogers's career after graduation from Penn State has enhanced her skills as a historic researcher, as she worked as the collections manager and also as preservation associate at the SS *United States Conservancy* and is pursuing a Master of Science degree in history at the University of

Edinburgh, Scotland. Evidence of Rogers's continuing interest in Bucks County history is her appointment to the Upper Southampton Historical Advisory Board, in addition to the Craven Hall Historical Society Board of Directors.

Jennifer Rogers has a genuine passion for discovering the stories of Bucks County's past, from the early days of the Lenni-Lenape Native Americans to the founding of Pennsylvania, to the Revolutionary War and forward to the more modern influences of Bucks County in art and theater. *Hidden History of Bucks County* should be a "must read" for all area history buffs.

—Dr. Ellen Andrews Knodt
English and American Studies
Penn State University–Abington

Acknowledgements

Growing up in Bucks County, Pennsylvania, I was quickly immersed in the historical beauty hidden across the county, just northeast of the city of Philadelphia. Bounded by the Delaware River—an influential piece of American history itself—Bucks County, one of Pennsylvania's first three counties, was founded in 1682 by prominent Quaker, philosopher and entrepreneur William Penn. Originally encompassing what is now Northampton and Lehigh Counties until 1752, Bucks became home to many notable figures and celebrities, quite a few making it into history books.

My passion for history was not always the strongest. It wasn't until my sophomore year at Pennsylvania State University that I discovered this newfound love, all thanks to professors Dr. Ellen Knodt, as well as Dr. James Adams, may he rest in peace. My family, especially my parents, Ray and Cindy; brother, Brian; sister-in-law, Mary; and fiancé, Tyler, has continued to support me through all of my historic endeavors, whether they believed I spread myself "too thin" or not—their encouragement has meant so much to me.

Becoming so involved with local history, beginning with the time I spent at Mercer Museum as an intern during undergrad, as board member of the Upper Southampton Township Historical Advisory Board and the Craven Hall Historical Society and through my research I conducted as part of this book, I have gained valuable knowledge of Bucks County's past. The plethora of history hidden within the still-standing stone walls,

Victorian-era archways and Underground Railroad station stops is overwhelming, so much so that it is near impossible to include in just one book. Doesn't it just make you wonder how much is left to uncover? Please allow me to guide the way as you navigate through this book, hopefully leaving you walking away with a better sense of Bucks's little known tales and stories.

Flourishing with an abundance of history dating back to the early 1600s, the original Bucks County residents have left quite an imprint on the structures and relics still existing today, and a huge thank-you goes out to the historians, librarians and curators and all those who share the same love for local history as I do. It has never been more important to preserve this county's history. As the construction of new buildings and homes continues, historic grounds and structures may sadly meet their tragic demise. It is up to us to save Bucks County's history. Here's to you.

THE FOUNDING OF BUCKS COUNTY

On August 31, 1682, William Penn (October 14, 1644–July 30, 1718) embarked on a voyage from Deal, England, across the Atlantic Ocean on the ship *Welcome* alongside many of Bucks County's future prominent figures. The *Welcome* was one of the twenty-two ships to cross the Atlantic bringing the first two thousand settlers to the Province of Pennsylvania between 1681 and 1682. Accompanied by one hundred immigrants, mostly Quaker Friends, *Welcome*'s passengers suffered through a long, dreary passage, leaving thirty dead from a smallpox outbreak on board the vessel. Penn endeared himself to all on board, paying close attention to the sick and dying. The crossing lasted fifty-seven days, with the *Welcome* anchoring at Upland (Chester, Pennsylvania) on October 28, 1682. Approximately half of those who arrived with William Penn settled here, and some of their descendants are still found scattered across the county, bearing the same names to this day.

Nearly four months before William Penn arrived in America, Penn's cousin William Markham made the first official purchase in Bucks County on July 15, 1682, using wampum, a few blankets, guns, beads and other miscellaneous goods to pay for the plot of land. In 1684, William Penn returned to England to manage his father's estate in County Cork, Ireland, and participated in military action against Irish rebels. Penn's father was granted the Macroom Castle estate, which had been originally owned by the MacCarthys. While it is unknown when Penn converted to Quakerism, the course of his life significantly changed when he heard a

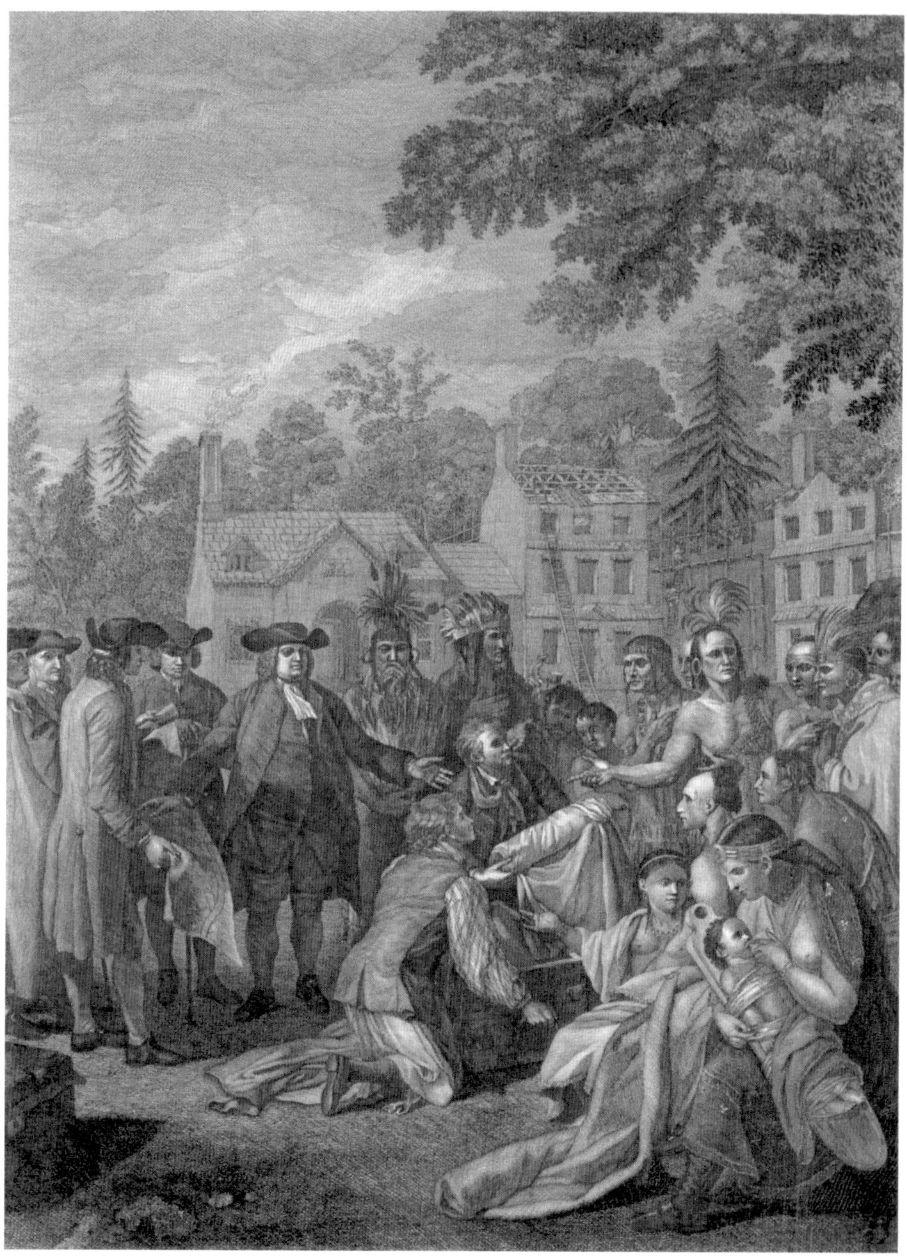

"Guillaume Penn Traite Avec Les Indiens." *Library of Congress, Prints and Photographs Division.*

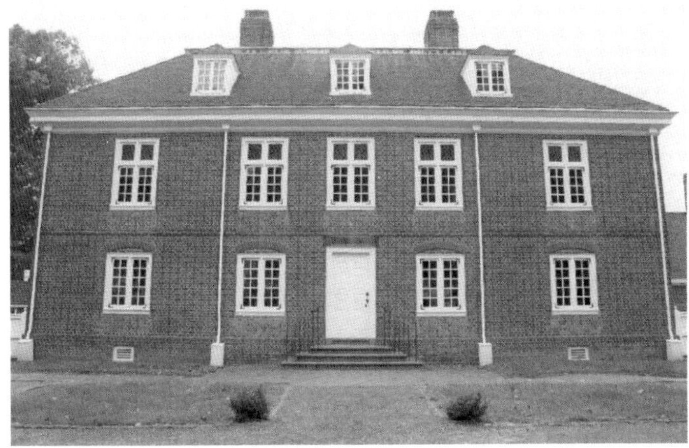

Pennsbury Manor.
Reconstructed
estate of William
Penn from 1683 to
1701. Penn spent
only a few years at
the estate.

Quaker preacher teaching the ideals of the religion. During this same time, the English Crown refused to allow new religious groups to rise under its rule, in turn, outlawing every religion other than the Church of England. Because of this outlandish ruling, Penn composed tracts, letters and books to further fight for freedom of religion. Quakerism would soon benefit under Penn's dedication to the religion through his remarkable talent and connections. William Penn's involvement in the Quaker lifestyle would later assist in the development of East Jersey and West Jersey, two Quaker colonies that were established by England. In 1680, he approached King Charles II of England, requesting land in America that would ignite a new nation. By designing a colony and government that would reflect his own personal views, Penn would become the proprietor of Pennsylvania just a short year later. William Markham, an English surveyor and soon-to-be deputy governor of the province, was sent to map out the city of Philadelphia based on a grid pattern with squares of open space. Markham would later choose the site of Penn's estate, now Pennsbury Manor in Morrisville, Bucks County, constructing his home in 1682.

Despite Penn being recognized as the founder of Quakerism in the Commonwealth of Pennsylvania, others, including Robert Wade, who immigrated to Chester from England, may have led the Quaker movement throughout Bucks County prior to Penn's arrival. Wade, a member of the Religious Society of Friends, was most likely the first Quaker to settle in Pennsylvania, assisting in the establishment of the Commonwealth's first Quaker meetinghouse in Chester. Another group of Quakers, the Falls Meeting, established in 1683, built the first meetinghouse in what is now

Fallsington, Bucks County, in 1690. The first settlers and founders of this meeting were granted tracts of land by the governor of New York and New Jersey, Sir Edmund Andros, prior to Governor Markham's arrival in 1681.

In 1681, while still in England, William Penn established a government in Pennsylvania based on the idea of granting individual rights, rather than one reflecting older forms of government. By emphasizing self-government for the people and rejecting forced laws on citizens, Penn drew more immigrants to the Commonwealth with his ideals of governing for the people, regardless of religious or ethnic differences, complete with a judicial system that in turn confirmed the role of juries. Nearly fifteen years later, an assembly of thirty-six men that had been elected to accept or reject proposed laws demanded the power to create them. Even though Penn disagreed, his desire to help the people of the Commonwealth was more important than his own opinions on government, changing Pennsylvania's government. His same ideals inspired the nation's founding fathers and, subsequently, the Constitution, and were continually referenced in documents throughout Pennsylvania history.

Beginning in the 1680s, hundreds of Europeans immigrated to Pennsylvania, predominantly those of English, Welsh, Scots-Irish, Irish and German descent. These same settlers, many of whom were Quakers, established meetinghouses throughout Bucks, Chester and Philadelphia Counties in order to create places for worship and education. Penn sought out settlers who possessed a range of skills to help build the colony, some assisting in the creation of the government. Wealthy immigrants became prominent figures in the Commonwealth; some settlers purchased slaves from Africa or the Caribbean, while middle-class colonists worked as small, independent business owners or free laborers. Those who were lower than the middle class mostly became indentured servants. Pennsylvania acted as a melting pot as it became a society made up of a multitude of ethnicities and economic backgrounds ranging from the Native Lenni-Lenapes to servants and wealthy landowners. Penn established a peaceful relationship with the Lenapes in the area, particularly in Bucks County, learning their native tongue and cooperating with the Native Americans' desires and needs.

Bucks County was primarily settled by families of three distinct nationalities—English, Scots-Irish and German. The Welsh would arrive shortly after the others, some settling in Middle and Upper Bucks County. The melting pot of settlers gave Bucks County its unique population. The English, who were mostly Quaker Friends, were among the first to arrive, many coming with or following William Penn. They settled throughout Bucks, Chester and Philadelphia Counties and would become the founders of the Commonwealth of Pennsylvania. The Germans followed, influencing areas near the Schuylkill and Delaware with their language and customs. The German settlers consisted of several denominations, particularly Lutheran, Reformed Christian and Mennonite. The Scots-Irish began to arrive in 1716. It is important to note that the Scots-Irish were not typically of Gael or Celt descent, but rather Scottish and primarily Presbyterian. The Catholic native Irish would arrive several years later. The Scots-Irish arrived in such large numbers that in 1729, James Logan, a County Armagh, Ireland–born Quaker who became Penn's secretary, said that it was beginning to look as if Ireland is sending "all her inhabitants to this Province." That year, 6,000 arrived with immigration commencing the first part of the eighteenth century. Some records suggest that between 250,000 and 400,000 Scots-Irish arrived in America in the eighteenth century. Many came to Bucks County in search of homes from the Neshaminy to the farthest points of Upper Bucks. Soon after their arrival, these same settlers would establish the first Presbyterian churches in the county. The native Irish Catholics arrived in great numbers due to the starvation and tragedy of the Irish Potato Famine, which began in 1845, when approximately 1.5 million starved to death. A million more fled to America to escape dire poverty, with many settling in the Philadelphia area, including Bucks County.

I

William Penn and the Lenni-Lenapes

Chief Tamanend of the Lenni-Lenape tribe in Bucks County conceived an agreement with William Penn in 1683, stating that the Native Americans and Europeans would live together in peace as long as the creeks and rivers would continue to flow through the area. Tamanend trusted Penn for his willingness to put differences aside and agree for a state of tolerance and freedom for all. The Lenni-Lenape chief, who lived in the forests between the Neshaminy and Pennypack Creeks, spoke an Algonkian language, far different than the Iroquois of the north. According to several records, the local Lenni-Lenape population to which Tamanend belonged consisted of anywhere from 2,500 to over 12,000 people. The tribe's land stretched through the area, across New Jersey and as far south as northern Delaware. When William Penn arrived in America in 1682, he took it upon himself to get to know the local Indian tribes, even learning to speak their native tongue. This ultimately led him to enter into negotiations with over 20 sachems, or Native American leaders, as no other Englishman could speak for the Lenape people.

In the spring of 1683, William Penn rode to a Lenni-Lenape village called the "Perkasie Indian Town" in what is now Hilltown Township, to meet with Tamanend's son Yaqueekhon. Penn was welcomed with open arms with a feast, dancing and singing to the sound of drums. Shortly thereafter, Penn earned the trust of the Indians and would attempt to establish peace between them and the European immigrants. His idea of property rights were exclusive and for personal use, far different than the Indians' ideas

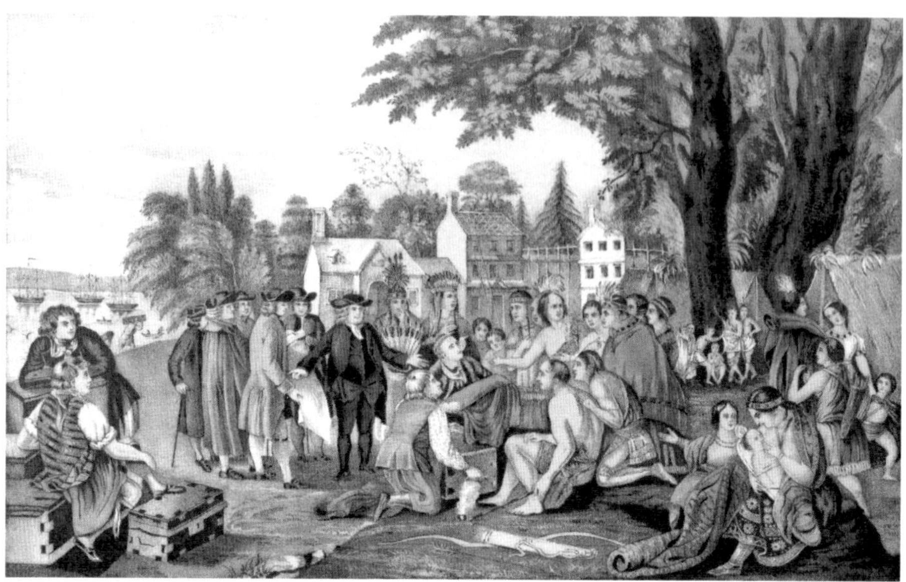

Penn's Treaty with the Indians at Shackamaxon, oil painting. Benjamin West, 1771. *From Pennsylvania Academy of the Fine Arts, Gift of Mrs. Sarah Harrison.*

that the land was of "our mother." However, Tamanend and the local sachems knew very little, if nothing at all, of the English legal system of deeds and land ownership. More meetings regarding the sale of property would continue to occur, usually ending with Penn assuring the Lenapes that they would not be pushed out of the area or treated unfairly. Once promised a strip of land on both sides of the Brandywine but later told that government officials were unable to locate the agreement, the Native Americans were rightfully apprehensive of Penn's promise. Regardless of their fears, Tamanend understood that the sale of land did not necessarily mean that the Indians would be pushed out of the area, and Penn, who instructed his surveyor to never disturb the Indian villages, gave him good reason to believe they could still hunt and gather as they had before.

In Philadelphia on June 23, 1683, William Penn and Captain Lasse Cock, a Swedish interpreter, were joined by Chief Tamanend and five sachems in Shackamaxon, or what is now Kensington. The meeting revolved around a deed of sale, leading to Tamanend granting the land between the Pennypack and Neshaminy Creeks to William Penn. Captain Lasse Cock and Tamanend both signed the deed, with Cock as the witness. During subsequent council meetings, some tensions arose between the two, however, the Native Americans and settlers continued to agree to peace and understanding between their people. It is estimated that Tamanend was deceased by the year 1701. During that same year, the Lenni-Lenapes sent a letter to the King of England expressing their high regard for William Penn.

2

BUCKS COUNTY

Bucks County, founded in November 1682, received its name from the county of Buckinghamshire of southeast England—Penn's family seat and home of many of the area's first settlers. The Pennsylvania county's earliest settlers hailed from Great Britain and Ireland. In fact, many of the towns and townships within the county were named after places in England and Ireland as a result of its first residents and explorers.

Bucks County inhabitants have experienced some of America's most influential battles, witnessed a dramatic shift in historic architecture and welcomed over 600,000 residents. However, the county is not just brimming with proud residents. With Philadelphia being a neighboring county, Bucks has seen thousands of visitors flock to the area, particularly for its history, nature and tourist attractions.

On January 5, 1681, the colony of Pennsylvania was confirmed to Penn under the great seal of England. In March, Penn received a royal charter for the Province of Pennsylvania, granted by King Charles II. He then proceeded to persuade people to immigrate to the new province, offering the terms of one hundred acres for forty shillings. With Pennsylvania consisting of approximately forty thousand square miles, Penn sought to divide the province into several counties, beginning with Bucks, Chester and Philadelphia Counties—the three original counties at the formation of Pennsylvania—just one year later.

In March 1683, in order to establish Penn's government, a number of acts were passed at the first Provincial Assembly in Philadelphia. The land

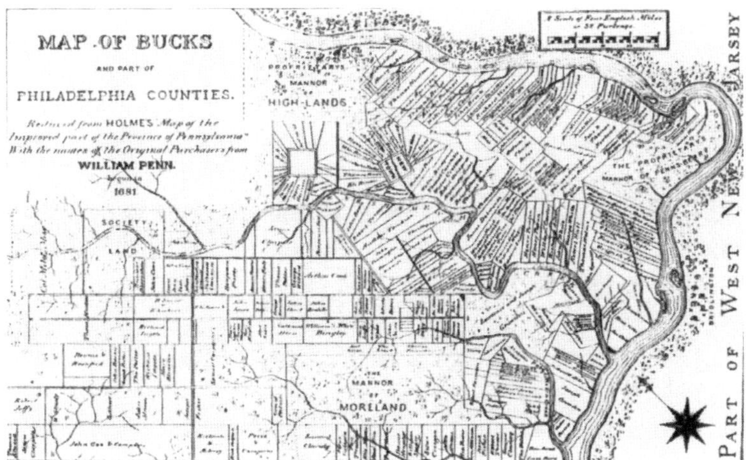

Map of Bucks County and parts of Philadelphia County based on the original created by Thomas Holme in 1681.

was divided into three counties, Philadelphia, Bucks and Chester—Bucks's boundaries began "at ye river Delaware, at Poaquesson creek, and so to take in the Easterly side thereof, together with ye townships of Southampton and Warminster, and thence backwards." The county was not declared "Bucks" for a few months following the assembly. The county line between Bucks and Philadelphia, which at the time also included Montgomery County, was approximately the same as we find it now. The council ordered that the seal of Bucks County be a "Tree and Vine."

In 1690, the first legal steps toward dividing the county into townships occurred when the Provincial Council authorized warrants to be drawn, handing power to magistrates and grand juries to divide the land into hundreds of subdivisions, if necessary. However, prior to 1690, some of these townships, or geographical subdivisions, were given the names that they currently bear—several years before these townships were declared so by law: Southampton and Warminster were named as early as 1685, when the council fixed the line between Bucks and Philadelphia Counties; Newtown and Wrightstown were first written of in 1687. Other early named communities include Falls Township, after the falls in Delaware; Newtown, as it was a "new town," or "Settlement in the woods"; and Middletown, "midway between the uppermost inhabitants and those on the river below." Other townships were named after places from which their settlers hailed, usually in England, as well as where friends or family lived. Southampton Township's original boundaries extended eastward to Bensalem Township. The land formerly belonged to Lenni-Lenape Chief Tamanend, who later deeded it to William Penn on June 23, 1683.

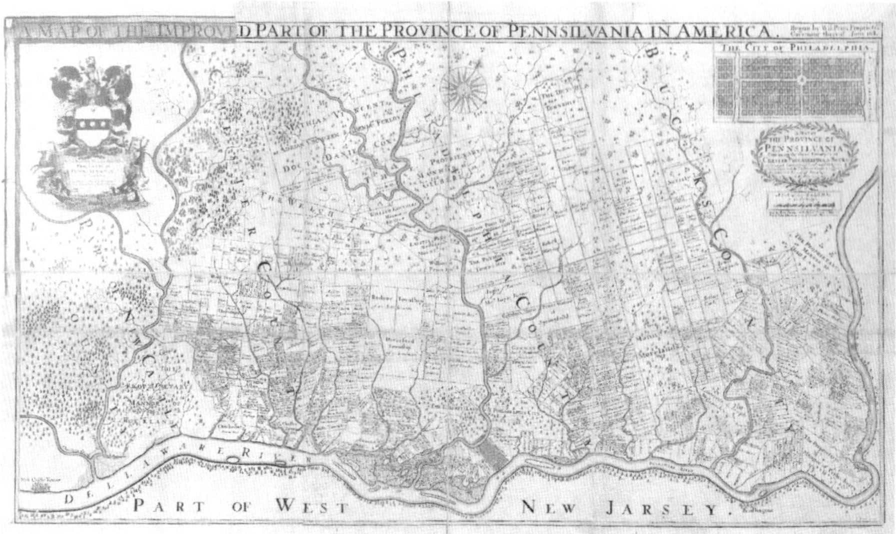

"A map of the improved part of the Province of Pennsylvania in America: Begun by William Penn, Proprietary & Governor thereof anno 1681." *Library of Congress, Geography and Map Division.*

In 1929, the township was divided into Upper Southampton and Lower Southampton.

Bucks County did not take advantage of this act until two years after it was instituted when the court, in September 1692, appointed a jury consisting of Provincial Judge Arthur Cook of Northampton, Joseph Growden, John Cook, Thomas Janney, Richard Hough, Henry Baker, Phineas Pemberton, Joshua Hoops, William Biles, Nicolas Walne, Edmund Lovet, Abraham Cox and James Boyden—all of whom were directed to meet at the Neshaminy Meeting House in Middletown Township. By the December term, the jury had concluded that the other settled areas in Bucks County would be divided into five townships: Makefield, Falls, Buckingham (originally named Greeneville), Bensalem (then Salem) and Middletown. However, Buckingham, as noted above, is not today's Buckingham between Doylestown and New Hope. The original Buckingham comprised approximately seventeen square miles near Falls. Within the township was the village of Bristol (founded in 1681), which was home to the county's only seaport, on the Delaware River. "Buckingham" and the seaport were officially incorporated as Bristol Borough in 1722. Falls Township, in particular, is sometimes known by historians as the original township. Within its borders, the first settlement was established, and with it came the first English civilization in Bucks. It was also here that William Penn, "the great founder," built his Bucks County home, which once stood where the historically accurate reconstructed Pennsbury Manor is today. Historian William Watts Hart Davis wrote in his book, *The History of Bucks County, Pennsylvania: From the Discovery of the Delaware to the Present Time*, that "the feet of many immigrants pressed its soil before they took up their march for the wilderness of Middletown, Newtown, and Wrightstown."

Several years before Penn arrived in the area, numerous families settled near present-day Falls. By the late 1630s, Falls was home to settlers from both Holland and Sweden, who were later driven out by the English. Surrounding areas were explored primarily by Native Americans outside of an occasional settler seeking refuge in the woods.

As an influential county during the American Revolution, Bucks witnessed the wisdom, patriotism and courage of the many men and women who led the revolt against the British, fought in horrific circumstances and provided hospice care to the injured and tended to the deceased. Several historic structures and landmarks that served as General George Washington's headquarters still stand today, and the tumultuous story of the Revolutionary War in Bucks County cannot be told often enough. On several occasions, the Continental Army and General Washington marched through Bucks County, setting foot on our very own township lands to greet the enemy and prepare for monumental battles. In 1776, General George Washington and his army marched through parts of Bucks County, but before they would reach New Jersey for the historic Battle of Trenton, they would have to make their way across the Delaware River through a severe wintry mix of snow and ice. Though these men had experienced an extremely tough loss in New York just a couple of months before the famous battle, they never gave up. If they hadn't persisted through the harsh northeastern winter conditions, then one of the most monumental battles of the Revolutionary War would not have been won and the cause for freedom may have been lost.

However, despite Washington's widespread support in Bucks County, a considerable minority of its population remained loyal to the British. When war became inevitable, Bucks County was one of the first to act in resistance to the Crown. Quakers were morally opposed to the war from the start due to the strife and bloodshed the conflict would bring to the thousands fighting in its battles. This did not prohibit some from lending a hand to the cause—a number entered the military service, while others could not forget the needs of charity.

The American Revolution caused thousands of deaths but ultimately led to the creation of thirteen independent states no longer under British rule and the founding of a new nation: the United States of America. Three signers of the Declaration of Independence resided in Bucks County—George Taylor, a colonel in the Bucks County Assembly; George Clymer, a prominent merchant from Morrisville; and Robert Morris, famed financier of the Revolution.

PART I

Prominent Families and Homesteads

Bucks County has been home to many famous award-winning authors, musicians and sports champions, but before they were born, the county's earliest settlers, as well as those who influenced the region centuries later, left monumental footprints in Bucks throughout their lifetimes. One of the county's oldest known records, titled *A Registry of All the People in the County of Bucks, in the Province of Pennsylvania, that Have Come to Settle the County,* written in 1684 by Phineas Pemberton, indicated that the first official register of Bucks County included seventy family names.

In 1682, the original county records showed that the first settlers in Bucks County primarily came from England, and many were therefore English Quakers. These early residents helped shape what Bucks County is today, and though there are far too many to explore thoroughly, some have left a valuable imprint in the community, while others were large landowners.

How our fathers lived in the then remote region of Bucks County, of what their wealth was composed, what they wrangled over, are topics upon which history consents to shed but a partial light. Nearly two hundred years have filled the gap between the arrival of Penn and his Quaker colony and the richly prosperous present. During the first century of this interval no literary remains of any importance touching the social life of the colonists are extant. Nothing reliable save a few legal records, dust-begrimed and almost illegible are left to tell who were the men who felled the trees and turned the soil in 1682.

—Bucks County Gazette, *August 28, 1873*

3

THE GRUNDY FAMILY

The Grundy family's ancestors were some of Bucks County's earliest European settlers—one of whom, Giles Knight, immigrated to America with William Penn aboard the ship *Welcome*. (Some records indicate that Giles Knight sailed on a different ship of the same fleet called *The Society*.) Edmund Grundy, a prominent merchant and citizen in the Philadelphia region, married Rebecca Hulme, whose mother, Rachel Knight, was a descendant of William Penn's possible shipmate Giles Knight.

Rebecca Hulme's father, William, also was a direct descendant of a notable figure in Bucks County, John Hulme, founder of Hulmeville, Pennsylvania. John Hulme became one of the most respected men in the county, was elected several times to the legislature and as the first president of the Farmers' Bank of Bucks County, and helped transform Hulmeville into an industrial town with cotton and woolen factories and a gristmill. William Grundy, father of Margaret and Joseph, was born in Philadelphia in 1836 and was the second son of Edmund and Rebecca Hulme Grundy. William held a powerful career in the wool trade, leading him to establish a worsted yarn manufacturing company in Philadelphia, Grundy Brothers and Campion. (It later moved operations to Bristol in 1876.) The Grundys resided in homes located throughout Bristol Borough until 1884, when they purchased and renovated the Grundy home that still stands today. William also served as burgess for the Borough of Bristol and was very active in improving the town, lobbying for the interests of American businesses and

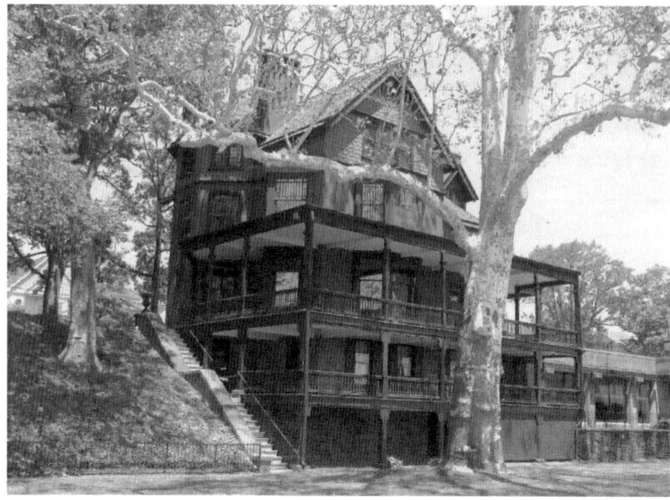

The Grundy Homestead, the Margaret R. Grundy Memorial Museum. First section built 1818. Additions added 1834 and again in 1884. Bristol, Bucks County.

protecting American industries. Margaret and Joseph were the two last direct descendants of Edmund Grundy and the Grundy family.

The family expanded the house, adding a two-story wraparound porch, a grand staircase and elegant wood and decorative details reflecting the Queen Anne style. The rooms are still adorned in the same fashion that the Grundy family would have left it over one hundred years ago.

4

THE THOMPSON FAMILY

John and Robert Thompson

John McGraudy Thompson, born on November 18, 1726, in County Tyrone, Ireland, moved to Bucks County alongside his three brothers, their mother, Elizabeth, uncle, Samuel, and several other families, including the Wilson family. Elizabeth, having been left a widow with her four sons, decided to immigrate to Penn's colony in America, accompanied by friends and relatives in the journey overseas. According to Thompson family records, Elizabeth's father begged her on his knees to remain in Ireland, pouring out an earnest prayer to preserve her and the rest of her family from a life in the wilderness and the perils of sea. There are records indicating that the Wilsons were from Four Mile Run (or Five Mile Stone), County Antrim, near Auger. Throughout the mid-1700s, much of the area between Warwick, Warrington, Newtown, Upper Makefield and Southampton welcomed Irish and Scots-Irish settlers, particularly near the Neshaminy Church of Warwick, established in 1727 near Wrightstown.

In 1753, Elizabeth's brother Samuel purchased a tract of three hundred acres of land in Warwick Township located near the property of two other prominent families, the Mearns and Ramseys (both later married the second generation of the Thompson family). The property had been held by land speculators up until Samuel's purchase, with records indicating that it remained a temporary home for Elizabeth and her four sons, John, Hugh, Robert and William, for several years.

JOHN THOMPSON

John, the youngest of the four brothers, joined William in the purchase of the mill site in Northampton Township in 1758. Being a miller by vocation, he likely learned his trade at the Mearns Mill in Warwick Township. A successful businessman, John became an even larger land owner when he purchased 79 acres and 148 perches of land connecting to the mill property. Robert Cummings conveyed another plantation with 109 acres, expanding the homestead and mill plot to total nearly 228 acres. The gambrel-roof house, which still stands today, was home to the Thompsons for many generations. Unfortunately, during the rise of the Doan Gang (more on these infamous brothers later), John's property was raided by the Tory-supporting outlaws who ransacked his house in search of money to support the British government and its army. Legend has it that John's wife, Mary, twin sister of William's wife, concealed their money in her seat cushion, refusing to leave the chair due to her frail and weak body, in turn saving their fortune.

John Thompson was an active Patriot who fought during the American Revolution, later enrolling himself as ensign of the Northampton Company of Associators, or military volunteers, and becoming Bucks County's first sheriff under the Constitution on March 22, 1777, serving until October 17, 1779. Thompson was appointed wagon master in January 1778, subagent for purchasing flour for the French fleet in July 1779 and collector of excise tax on October 20, 1783. Being that he held a position as a commissioned officer as well as the fact that he had funds collected for government use readily available, it is likely that he became a target for the Doan Gang, as the brothers usually directed their attention toward tax collectors.

At his death in July 1799, John was one of Bucks County's largest landowners with nearly one thousand acres to his name. According to his will, John was buried in the Presbyterian Graveyard in Newtown and split his land among his six sons. John Thompson's house, on Second Street Pike just outside of Richboro, Bucks County, is known as the hip roof house, despite having an elongated gambrel roof. The house, built in 1740, was listed in the National Register of Historic Places in July 1973.

ROBERT THOMPSON

Robert Thompson, born in November 1722, the second oldest of the Thompson brothers, became a miller like his brother John and lived most of his life in Wrightstown, Upper Makefield, before moving to New Hope. According to family documentation, local Quaker miller John Simpson operated nearby Neely's Mill at Pidcock's Creek in Solebury Township. Simpson would make Thompson a journeyman miller at his gristmill within just a few years.

One of Bucks County's first pioneers was John Pidcock. Pidcock frequently traded furs along the Delaware River and established a trading post with local Native Americans in 1684. He was the original owner of a five-hundred-plus-acre tract of land called Win-Na-Haw-Caw-Chunk by the Indians, near Pidcock Creek. Nearly fifty years later, John Simpson acquired the land and established the first gristmill in the area. About six months after Robert Thompson began working at Neely's Mill, Simpson passed away, leaving his widow Hannah Delaplaine and Robert to be married. The homestead, presently known as the Thompson-Neely House, was originally constructed by Simpson in about 1740 with additions made on its west end by Robert Thompson in 1757. A few years later, Robert's daughter Elizabeth married Irish immigrant William Neely, prompting her father to build a second story above the original section of the house. The Thompson and the Neely families were all living in the same house when over 7,400 Continental Army troops encamped in the nearby area, now known as Washington Crossing,

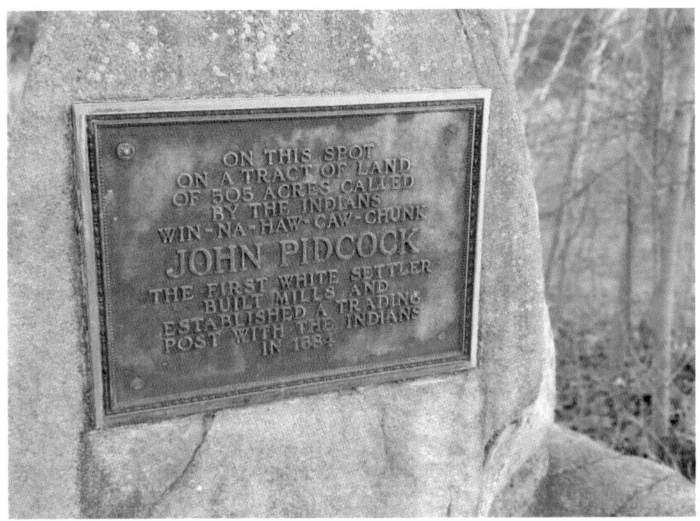

Marker indicating land once belonging to John Pidcock. Near Thompson-Neely House, remarking on trading post "on this spot" with Indians in 1684. New Hope, Bucks County.

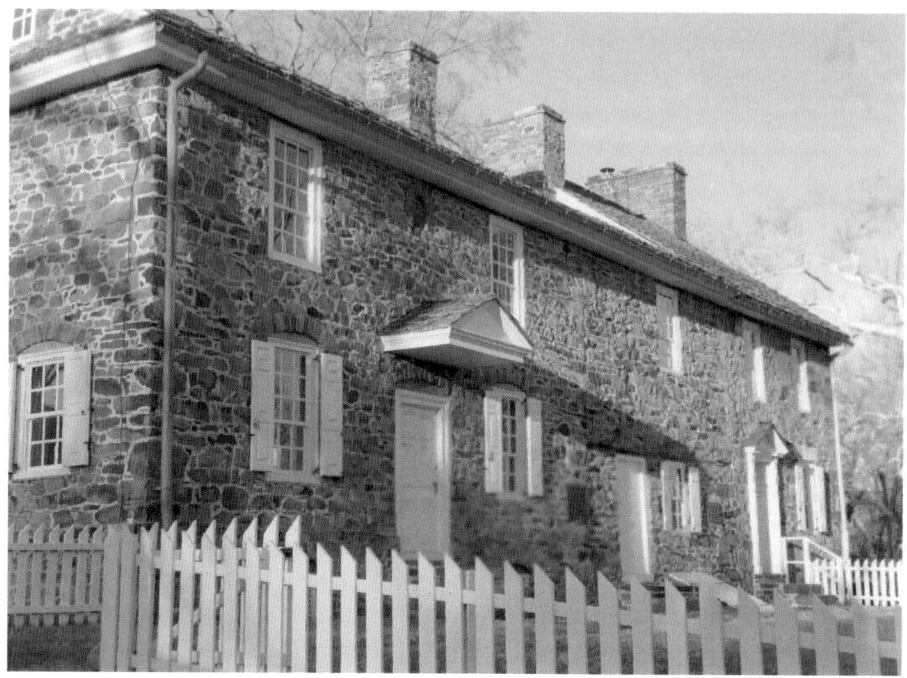

Thompson-Neely House. Eighteenth-century home, New Hope, Bucks County.

during the winter of 1776. As the homestead was a temporary army hospital during the winter campaign, many injured and sick soldiers were brought to the house for treatment and recovery; however, some reports state that many also lost their lives here. Among those injured in the line of duty during this campaign and treated at the house include James Monroe, who later became the fifth president of the United States; William Washington, cousin of General Washington; and Captain James Moore of the New York Artillery, who died of camp fever, along with others who died of exposure, disease and previous injury. Moore and several unidentified soldiers are buried on the property in what is now the Soldiers' Graves area, which is accessible to the public. Robert enlarged the house once more by adding the two-story east wing in 1788 to accommodate his growing family. Robert's milling business made him one of the wealthiest men in Solebury.

The Thompson-Neely House attained historical significance due to the crucial role it played during the Continental Army's winter encampment. The house is located on River Road between Washington Crossing and New Hope.

5

THE CRAVENS

Craven Hall, built in several stages during the end of the eighteenth century and early to mid-nineteenth century, is a stately Greek Revival home located on the southeast corner of Street and Newtown Roads in Warminster, Bucks County. In 1681, the land surrounding the homestead was part of a 500-plus-acre land grant from William Penn to William Bingley. At some point during the next forty-five years, William Stockdale acquired the land and then sold 150 acres to Jacobus James Craven in 1726 that remained in the Craven family until the death of Giles Craven in 1798. Before his death, Giles arranged for the land to be sold to Harman Vansant, grandson of Alice Craven. The homestead and land belonged to the Vansants until 1871. Despite the date of the initial construction of the house being unknown, the architectural details and local tax records indicate that it was built between 1790 and 1815, with the main wing being added in the mid-nineteenth century.

The Cravens were immigrants from Holland, many arriving in the eighteenth century. Jacobus James Craven was one of the trustees of the Neshaminy Presbyterian Church of Warwick in 1743. Jacobus became a large landowner in Moreland Township, Montgomery County, as well as in Warminster. In 1760, Jacobus died of old age. His children were Thomas, Giles, James, Alice (who would become wife of Harman Vansant), Elinor (wife of Clement Dungan), Hannah (wife of William McDowell), Esther (wife of William Gilbert) and Mary (wife of Anthony Scout). Thomas married Lena Bennett (whose family owned the Bennett-Search House in

Northampton Township) and then settled in Warminster on the Craven estate with sons William, James, Giles, Isaac and Thomas and daughters Christiana (wife of Thomas Beans), Edith (wife of Charles Vansant), Ann, Catharine and Helena. Isaac Craven inherited what is now known as Craven Hall, also sometimes referred to as "The Mansion House," as well as over one hundred acres of land in the township that had belonged to Jacobus. Isaac's children were William, Isaac, Abraham and Elenah (wife of John Finney). Abraham and Elenah survived their father and inherited his land. Abraham married Hannah Finney and settled in Moreland, Montgomery County, later returning to Warminster in 1882 following the death of his father.

Anna Eliza, the last surviving Vansant, sold Craven Hall to another relative, Isaac Bennett, whose family resided there until the 1920s. During the 1940s, the Lojeske family, who had a commercial vegetable operation on the land, offered two Japanese American families residencies following their release from an internment camp after World War II.

One of the other Craven family homesteads, located between Street and County Line Roads, was mentioned in several reports from the Battle of Crooked Billet, possibly the only Revolutionary War battle fought in Bucks County. The battle, which began in Hatboro, Montgomery County, continued into the neighboring county of Bucks, touching several areas, including Warminster, immediately adjacent to Hatboro. Records indicate that many of those wounded in battle, all under command of General John Lacey of the Continental Army, were carried into a dwelling owned by the Cravens on May 1, 1778. Lacey's troops suffered severe casualties and retreated across Thomas Jones's farm to the house. Twenty-six men were killed and numerous were missing, perhaps captured.

Lacey and his men marched across the farm of Thomas Craven in what was then the village of Johnsville, moving toward Hart's Corner on Bristol Road in an effort to escape the rapidly approaching Lieutenant Colonel John Graves Simcoe and the Queen's Rangers. Lacey's troops moved across York Road through Hartsville, hoping to come in from behind to catch the enemy off guard.

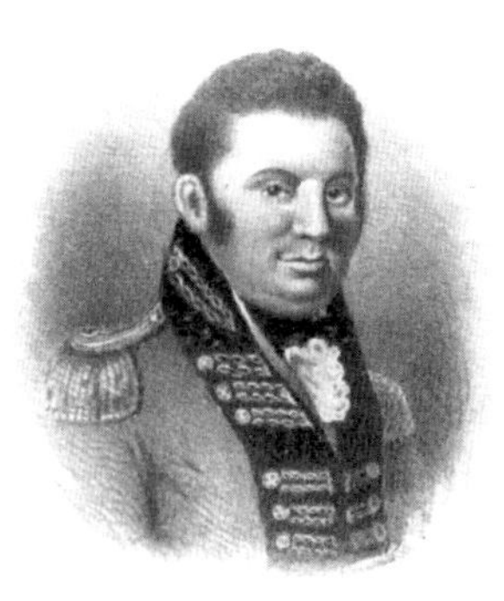

John Simcoe, lieutenant colonel commandant of the Queen's Rangers. 1880. *New York Public Library, Emmet Collection.*

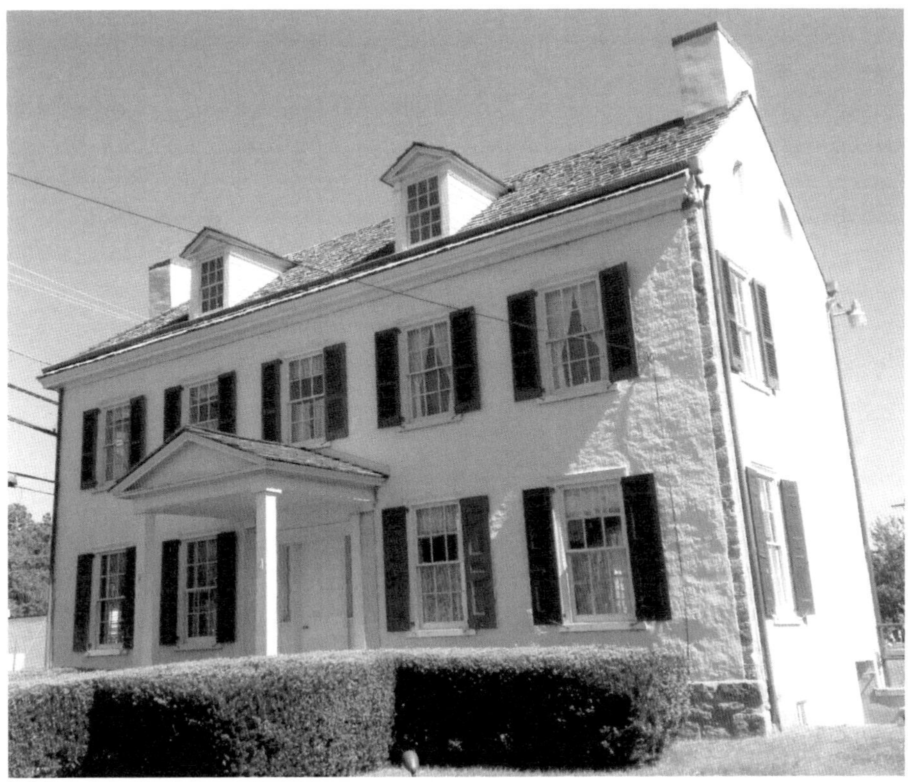

Craven Hall, Warminster, Bucks County. Built in stages in the mid- to late eighteenth century. *Craven Hall Historical Society.*

Upon their arrival, Lacey found many of his own men killed and severely wounded, some of whom were brutally murdered. Simcoe followed the American soldiers until they made a sudden left, causing the British to give up on their pursuit and begin raiding the houses in the village for bread, cheese and other rations. A few of the Queen's Rangers ventured to the residence of David Marple, grandfather of Colonel David Marple, ordering him to catch, cook and serve chickens for them. Marple was physically unable to do this, so they ordered his children to serve the meal, to which they complied.

The deceased were buried in a single grave in a field near County Line Road and Madison Avenue. The wounded were cared for at the Craven house until they recovered and were able to return to their homes. After ensuring that the injured were well taken care of, Lacey set up camp on the north bank of the Neshaminy Creek near Hartsville.

In 1952, Centennial School District purchased over seventy acres of the land that included Craven Hall and the neighboring family cemetery to build a high school. During its ownership of the property, Craven Hall was used as a junior high school and later administrative offices for the district. Unfortunately, the house deteriorated rather quickly and was subsequently abandoned in the mid-1970s. Centennial School District came to an agreement with what would be known as the Craven Hall Historical Society, formerly led by Ella Rhodes, to lease the dwelling to the nonprofit group. Restoration efforts were immediately underway and have continued with the help of volunteers and a board of directors.

6

HENRY MERCER

Henry Mercer, an innovative archaeologist, artifact collector and tile maker, was born in Doylestown on June 24, 1856. During his lifetime, Mercer designed three poured-concrete structures in Doylestown: Fonthill, the Moravian Pottery and Tile Works and Mercer Museum, all of which were built on sixty acres of land. Henry Mercer attended Harvard University from 1875 through 1879 and obtained his liberal arts degree from the prestigious school. He later continued his education at the University of Pennsylvania Law School in 1880 but never practiced in the field. Mercer became the founder of the Bucks County Historical Society that same year. For several years thereafter, Mercer traveled through Europe, particularly Germany and France.

In the 1890s, the University of Pennsylvania appointed Henry Mercer as its museum's curator of American and prehistoric archaeology. A few years later, after departing from his position at the museum, Mercer dedicated his life to locating and preserving historic American artifacts and learning the art of German-style pottery. In 1898, Mercer founded the Moravian Pottery and Tile Works after becoming an apprentice to a Pennsylvania/German potter. He was reportedly influenced by the American Arts and Crafts movement, which stood for traditional craftsmanship involving medieval, romantic or folk decorations and ultimately advocated for social reform. Mercer's tiles are used throughout the state, including in the floor of the Pennsylvania Capitol in Harrisburg. Other Mercer tiles can be found at the Casino de Monte-Carlo in Monaco, the St. Louis Public Library and the Rockefeller Estate in New York.

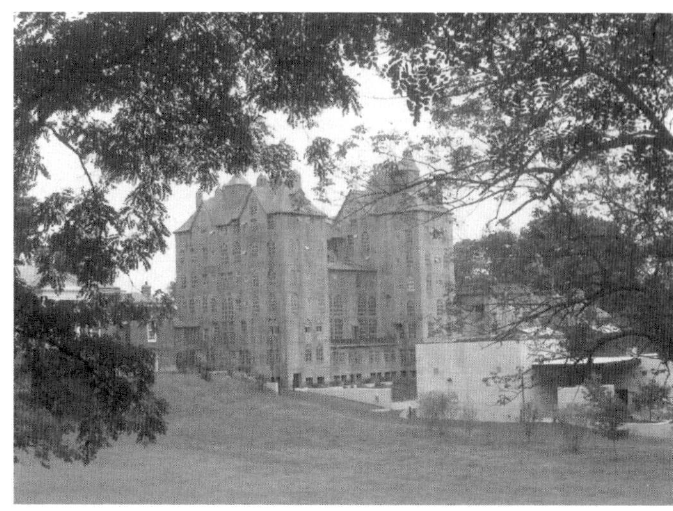

Mercer Museum, Doylestown, Bucks County.

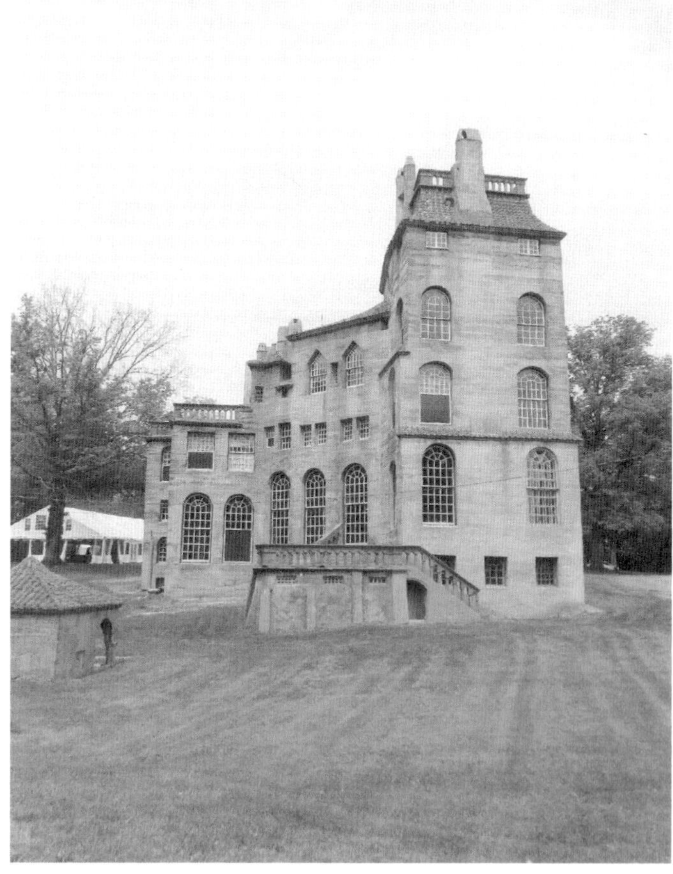

Fonthill Castle, Henry Mercer. Doylestown, Bucks County.

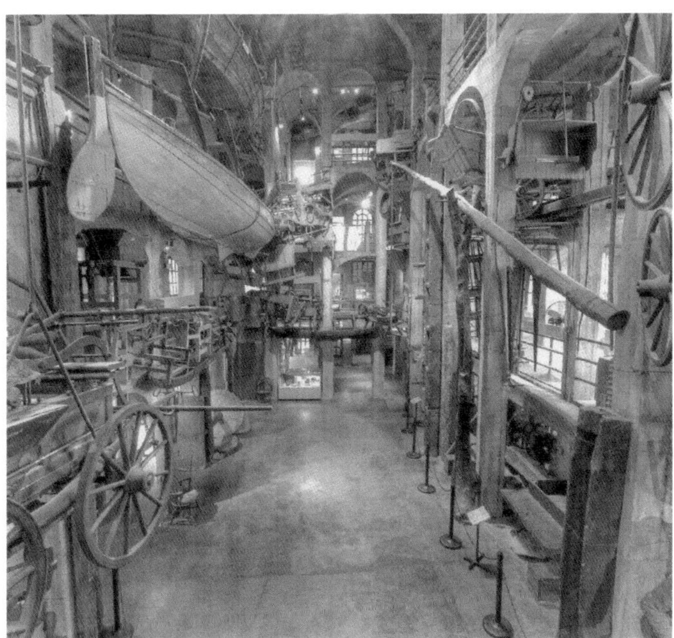

Mercer Museum interior, hanging artifacts. Doylestown, Bucks County.

Fonthill, which contains forty-four rooms, including ten bathrooms, five bedrooms and eighteen fireplaces, was built between 1908 and 1912. Despite the exterior of his home resembling a castle, Mercer decided the house was not going to be dark and gloomy indoors and therefore added two hundred windows to welcome in natural light. Fonthill was decorated with Mercer's own tiles but also included many Persian, Dutch, Spanish and Chinese tiles he had collected over the years. Equipped with an elevator and intercom buzzer, the home, even with its castle-like style, was incredibly modern. There are over nine hundred prints and artwork from his collection spread throughout the house.

In 1913–14, construction began on the seven-story Mercer Museum with the help of Lucy the horse and eight laborers. Taking three years to complete, the structure was constructed entirely of concrete reinforced with iron rods. Mercer used the seventeen-thousand-square-foot building to house and showcase over forty thousand artifacts, some of which hang from the museum's ceiling. The oldest artifacts include a two-thousand-year-old whale oil lamp and Native American tools and instruments dating to approximately 6,000 BC.

7

JOHN LACEY

It will not avail me to brag of high origin, but I can estimate my Ancestors among the first and most enterprising settlers of North America, who regardless of [torn] expanded and boisterous ocean, 8000 miles to seek in the wilds of North America among savage Indians an [asylum] where they might worship that Omnipotent being who rules according to the dictates of their own [consciences], which were forbidden them in their native Country. They were all of the society of Quakers, at that time sorely persecuted on that account in England. They were all freemen, and at least independent in their resources, if not rich or of noble blood. They were Companions of William Penn, the founder of Pennsylvania, who was of the same Religious profession. To encounter the perils of such an undertaking at so early a period of the settlement of this Country, at once bespeaks them to be a People not easily daunted at trifles, and by the conflicting elements, or of limited enterprise.
—*The* Pennsylvania Magazine of History and Biography *25*, Memoirs of Brigadier-General John Lacey, of Pennsylvania.

General John Lacey, born on February 4, 1755, to a Quaker family, was employed at his father's gristmill throughout childhood and became an American military officer during the American Revolutionary War. Appointed a brigadier general by the Pennsylvania Supreme Executive Council in January 1778, Lacey first served as a lieutenant colonel in the Bucks County Regiment during the Battles of Germantown and Matson's Ford just a year prior. As a native of Buckingham Township, Bucks County,

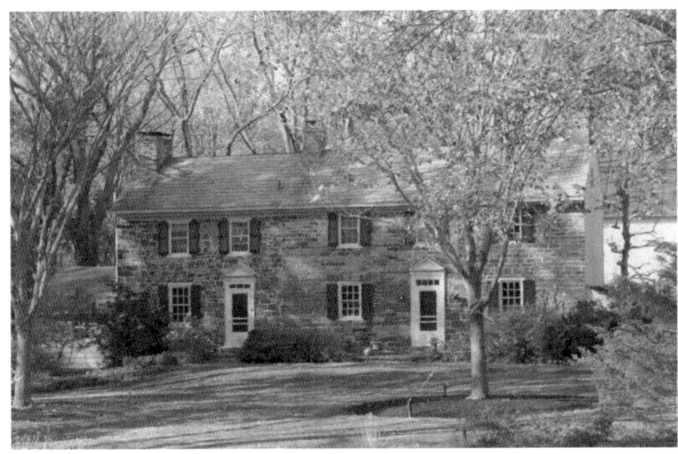

General John Lacey's homestead, Wycombe, Buckingham Township, Bucks County. Earliest known constructed section of house was completed in 1755.

Lacey's homestead was located in the Wycombe section of the township.

In 1776, General Lacey served as a captain under Colonel Anthony Wayne on the Canadian frontier. Lacey and Wayne fought often, leading Lacey to resign his commission and not return to service for a year. After his reenlistment, Lacey served as the Bucks County Regiment's lieutenant colonel and would later be promoted to brigadier general of the Pennsylvania Militia. Lacey would soon lead his troops in the Battle of Crooked Billet, fought in present-day Hatboro, Montgomery County, and areas of Warminster, Bucks County.

While General George Washington was encamped at Valley Forge during the winter of 1777, he ordered that the Pennsylvania Militia safeguard the northern region above Philadelphia in order to prevent farmers in nearby Philadelphia and Bucks Counties from exchanging farm goods for gold with British-occupied Philadelphia. The militia was also ordered to defend the counties' residents who were sympathetic to the Americans from any British raiders who sought to capture local Patriots and destroy American property.

At the start of the British occupation of Philadelphia, commander of the Pennsylvania Militia Brigadier General James Potter requested a leave of absence in January 1778. The Supreme Executive Council approved Potter's request, prompting a search for his replacement. On January 7, 1778, the council voted to appoint John Lacey as commander, including a promotion to brigadier general. Shortly thereafter, Lacey received a letter from the president of the council, Thomas Wharton, informing him of his recent appointment and promotion. At the time, Lacey was just twenty-five years old.

I received your favour dated the 21ˢᵗ Instant and must request that you will exert yourself to fulfil the intention of keeping a body of Troops in the Country where you are posted. Protecting the Inhabitants is one of the ends designed, and preventing supplies and intercourse with the Enemy is the other, this, perhaps with the utmost vigilance cannot be totally effected. But I must intreat [sic] you to take every step, that may render it possible. As to the reduction of your Numbers, I wish you to make timely application to the President of your State, to keep up the necessary force under your Command.

—letter from General George Washington
to Brigadier General John Lacey, January 23, 1778

Within a few weeks following his promotion, Brigadier General John Lacey was ordered in charge of the patrols, as per General Washington's request. By late April, General Lacey had established his headquarters near the Crooked Billet Tavern in Hatboro, Montgomery County. According to several reports, the British sent spies to the area to watch Lacey and his troops, as he was one of the most successful brigadier generals in the area prior to the skirmish at Crooked Billet. On April 30, over 800 men under General James Abercrombie and John Graves Simcoe marched out of Philadelphia toward Hatboro to attack Lacey and his militia, consisting of only about 150 to 400 men, most of whom were untrained and under armed. Simcoe with his 325 men, and Abercrombie with the main force of over 500, were guided by Loyalist spies familiar with the area. Throughout its encampment in Hatboro, Lacey's group frequently changed in size and began to dwindle. Despite being promised a minimum of 1,000 men, Lacey could only rely on a few hundred at his disposal, a number small compared to those he would face at the Battle of Crooked Billet. On that same night, several hours before the ambush, Lacey sent instructions to several subordinates to keep watch for any British movements or suspicious activity. Despite his instructions, Lieutenant William Neilsen reportedly did not follow orders to scout between two and three o'clock in the morning, causing him to run into Simcoe's men as they approached the unarmed camp. Lacey, who was sleeping in a nearby house near present-day York Road, awoke from the loud clashes from the skirmish—the British were just a short two hundred yards away. Knowing that they could not survive, Lacey ordered his men to retreat into an open field and a nearby wooded area. Nearly all of his men were either wounded or brutally killed by Simcoe's vicious forces.

Over a five-month period, Brigadier General Lacey was unable to accomplish any of the tasks Washington assigned to him, and the Pennsylvania Militia was ultimately ineffective against the British troops

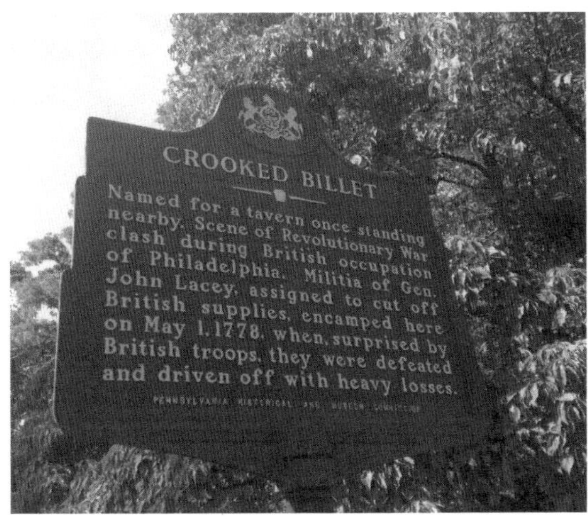

Battle of Crooked Billet historical marker, Hatboro, Montgomery County, Pennsylvania.

in Bucks County. General George Washington became displeased with Lacey's command, and much to his ease, General Potter returned just a month later, relieving General Lacey of his duties. Lacey placed blame on others, especially over the fact he was lacking in men by nearly 50 percent, stating that issue arose during his campaign from the lack of council and inadequate circumstances. General Lacey was certainly right in that he did not have full support of the state at the time—the fact he was promised one thousand men and only given a few hundred speaks volumes. However, the state was in chaos—Philadelphia had been captured, and the countryside, including Bucks County, had been raided by the British troops. With little revenue flowing in and Westmoreland and Cumberland Counties (Pennsylvania) under attack by the Native Americans, General Lacey was on his own. It can be argued, though, that another, more experienced commander would have defeated Simcoe and Abercrombie's troops at the Battle of Crooked Billet.

Following the Battle of Crooked Billet, Lacey was relieved of his command by George Washington, and he later died at the age of 59 on February 17, 1814.

Several communities were named in honor of General Lacey, including Lacey Park in Warminster and Lacey Township, New Jersey. The Lacey Homestead was built in six sections over the course of two hundred years, the earliest being constructed in the mid-eighteenth century. The house consisted of two and a half fieldstone sections with slate roofs, one half-story plaster and stone section, one half-story enclosed porch and a half-story framed section with a gable roof.

8

JOHN FITCH

Mr. Rumsey…at that time applying to the Assembly for an exclusive Act…spoke of the effect of Steam and…its application for the purpose of inland Navigation; but I did not conceive…that it was suggested as part of his original plan.…It is proper however for me to add, that some time after this Mr. Fitch called upon me on his way to Richmond and explaining his scheme, wanted a letter from me, introductory of it to the Assembly of this State the giving of which I declined; and went so [far] as to inform him that tho' I was bound not to disclose the principles of Mr. Rumsey's discovery I would venture to assure him, that the thought of applying steam for the purpose he mentioned was not original but had been mentioned to me by Mr. Rumsey.
—letter from George Washington to Thomas Johnson, November 22, 1787

John Fitch, American entrepreneur, inventor and engineer, was born on January 21, 1743, to Joseph Fitch and Sarah Shaler in Windsor, Connecticut, on a farm in what is now South Windsor, Connecticut. Fitch received some early education and became an apprentice to a clockmaker. In December 1767, John Fitch married Lucy Roberts and would open a rather unsuccessful brass foundry in his hometown and later a brass and silversmith company in Trenton, New Jersey. His foundry business was in operation for eight years until it was destroyed by British troops during the American Revolutionary War. Several years later, after moving to Warminster, Fitch would become famous for building the first steamboat in the country.

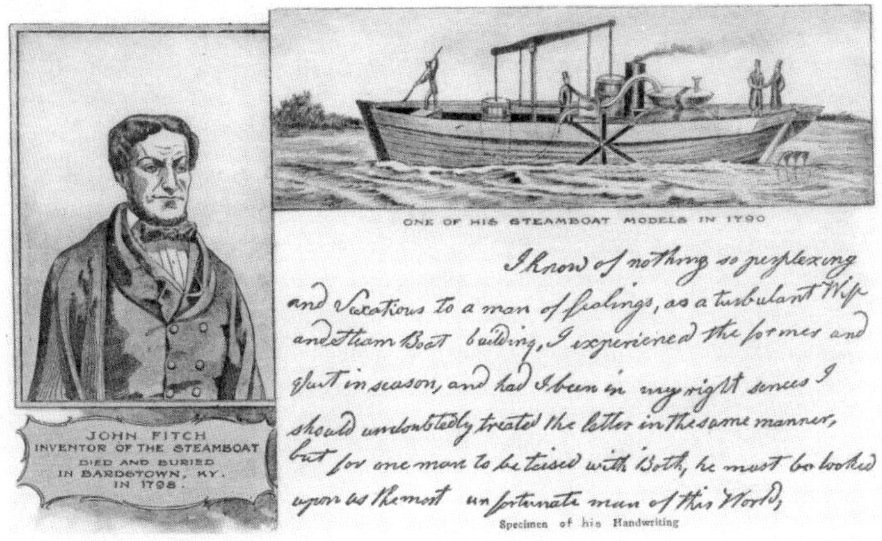

Postcard illustration of John Fitch, inventor of the steamboat, and one of his steamboat models. *Postcard Collection, Explore UK, the University of Kentucky.*

During the American Revolution, Fitch served as a gunsmith and armorer for the New Jersey Militia, later leaving his unit after a dispute over promotion. However, Fitch would continue to repair and refit artillery out of Trenton. In 1777, John Fitch provided liquor, rum and various supplies and rations to the troops stationed at Valley Forge. In 1780, he became a surveyor in Kentucky, claiming 1,600 acres for himself. While surveying in the Northwest Territory, which encompassed pre–Revolutionary War British territory north of the Ohio River, as well as areas in Illinois County and French Canada below the Great Lakes, Fitch was captured by Native Americans and turned over to the British. Shortly after his capture, he was released.

In the early 1780s, John Fitch moved to Warminster following his career as a surveyor. Despite the community being in its early stages at the time, it was here Fitch began his design of a steam-powered boat in 1785. After his first attempt at raising funds for the production of the vessel through the support of the Continental Congress, Fitch persuaded several state legislatures to grant him a fourteen-year monopoly for steamboat traffic on inland waterways, including rivers and canals. With this, Fitch was able to secure funds from prominent figures and businessmen in the city of Philadelphia.

John Fitch recalled seeing a drawing of a British Newcomen atmospheric engine—structures used to pump water from mines— and he would use the same principles in the design of his steamboat. Fitch had also heard of the Scottish steam engine developed by James Watt in the 1770s. Fitch was able to combine the ideas behind the Newcomen and Watt engines despite England preventing the export of any new technology to America following the Revolutionary War. Robert Fulton's 1807 steamboat, *Clermont*, would become the first years later. After moving to Philadelphia, Fitch was able to design his very own version of the steam engine, recruiting local clockmaker Henry Voigt to assist in the production of the working model. After he ran several test runs in a small creek in Southampton Township near what is now the intersection of Davisville and Street Roads, Fitch's first successful trial run was completed on the Delaware River on August 22, 1787. The trial run of steamboat *Perseverance* was made in front of delegates from the Constitutional Convention. (The Constitutional Convention, also known as the Grand Convention at Philadelphia, occurred from May 25 through September 17, 1787, in Philadelphia. George Washington's intention, along with James Madison's and Alexander Hamilton's, was to revise the Articles of Confederation. The result was the United States Constitution.) The *Perseverance* was propelled by several oars on the sides of the boat. Fitch and Voigt would continue to develop even better designs, and in June 1790, the pair launched a sixty-foot steamboat powered by an engine driving several stern-mounted oars. The oars paddled in a fashion similar to the motion of duck's feet. (An example of the early model can be found on display at Craven Hall in Warminster.) This version carried up to thirty passengers and traveled from Philadelphia to Burlington, New Jersey, during the summer of 1790. Fitch would claim that his steamboat would travel nearly 500 miles without mechanical problems, and estimates of miles traveled in the summer alone ranged from 1,300 to 3,000. The steamboat is said to have traveled at 6 miles per hour during rough conditions and upward of 8 miles per hour.

On August 26, 1791, John Fitch was granted a U.S. patent after a feud with rival steamboat inventor James Rumsey of Bath, Virginia, present-day Berkeley Springs, West Virginia. The recently established federal Patent Commission did not award Fitch his requested monopoly patent and instead gave him a modern patent for his latest design. The commission also awarded patents related to the steam engine on August 26 to Rumsey, Nathan Read of Massachusetts and John Stevens of New Jersey. Unable to secure the monopoly and the patent awards, Fitch's investors left his company. Even though his boats were successful in operation, Fitch was no longer able to continue his endeavor financially.

Nearly twenty years later, Robert Fulton would turn Fitch's idea into profitable success. Despite his ability to receive a monopoly in New York because of his powerful connection with partner Robert Livingston, Fulton was unable to obtain a U.S. patent due to his inability to demonstrate the steamboat's originality. William Thornton, a member of John Fitch's company, was able to make Fulton's patent application difficult, as he was head of the Patent Office. By 1791, John Fitch had also received a patent from France, and with the help of American investor Aaron Vail, he began to see a light at the end of the tunnel. Upon his arrival to France, Fitch was forced to abandon his plans, as the Reign of Terror, a period during the French Revolution, commenced. After attempting to patent his steamboat in London and failing, Fitch returned to the United States in 1794. He moved to Bardstown, Kentucky, several years later. Fitch hoped he could use his proceeds from the sale of land he acquired during the 1780s to build a steamboat; however, when he arrived, Fitch found settlers occupying his property, resulting in legal disputes. While in Kentucky, Fitch continued working on his steam engine designs, prompting him to build two models, one of which was lost to a fire in Bardstown; the other was found in his daughter's house in Ohio in 1849. Today, the latter is housed at the Ohio Historical Society Museum in Columbus. Apparently, according to a curator from the Smithsonian Museum in the mid-twentieth century, the model is actually a "prototype of a practical land-operating steam engine" or, in other words, a steam locomotive. Fitch sadly lost his will to live and passed away on July 2, 1798. He is buried in Bardstown.

9

WILLIAM WATTS HART DAVIS

William Watts Hart Davis, also known as William W.H. Davis, was a highly educated local historian, having a broad education from an early age through his military career. William, born on July 27, 1820, in Southampton Township, Bucks County, to Major General John Davis and Amy Hart Davis, would become one of the county's most influential figures in regards to documenting its history. William was educated as a child at a local private school led by Anna Longstreth before enrolling at the Southampton Baptist Church classical school. In 1832, Davis continued his studies at the academy in Doylestown before completing his early education at a boarding school in Burlington, New Jersey. At just age ten, Davis began his military career in a militia unit called the Liberty Guards—a company composed of young men from Northampton, Southampton and Warminster Townships, commanded by Captain Hugh Thompson. The Liberty Guards frequently met for drill at Bear Tavern—a local inn that was located in present-day Richboro, Bucks County. The Liberty Guards was attached to the First Regiment Bucks County Volunteers and was disbanded before the American Civil War. As an adult, William Davis studied at Norwich University in Vermont, and following his graduation, he was appointed the Military School in Portsmouth, Virginia's military instructor, as well as math teacher, and he was employed there for three years. Prior to studying law at Harvard University in 1846, William Davis worked for Judge John Fox in Doylestown. Davis enlisted in the Mexican-American War as a private in the First Massachusetts Infantry and was commissioned first lieutenant of Captain Crowningshield's Company in December of that year. He was mustered out in July 1848.

During the American Civil War, William Davis raised his own regiment—the 104th Pennsylvania Volunteers—on August 21, 1861, taking the oath of allegiance before Squire John Pugh of Doylestown. Davis gathered and trained his troops and soon led them into battle. In Washington, D.C., Davis was placed in command of a brigade consisting of the 56th New York, 52nd Pennsylvania, as well as his own 104th. On Saturday, May 31, 1862, Davis and his 104th Regiment experienced one of their most deadly encounters on the outskirts of Richmond, Virginia, against the defenders of the city. During the Siege of Charleston, General Davis was struck in the hand by an exploding shell and lost several of his fingers. Once he recovered from his wounds, Davis was ordered to sit on the General Court Martial Board in Philadelphia. On March 13, 1865, due to his prior outstanding military career, Davis was brevetted to brigadier general.

In the years after the Civil War, Davis played a pivotal role in securing funds for the construction of the 104th Pennsylvania Volunteer Regiment monument in Doylestown center, as well as organizing reunions and gatherings for his former troops. The gatherings were held at local venues and taverns from Quakertown to Hartsville. General Davis's opinions following the Civil War were far different than those of President Lincoln. In a letter to Harrisburg's Fourth of July Celebration committee, Davis wrote that "conciliation and generosity [should] be the ruling policy; let the people of the South be treated as erring citizens and not as implacable foes.…[L]et justice everywhere be largely tempered with mercy."

General Davis ran as a Democratic candidate for Congress in both 1882 and 1884, unsuccessfully. Under Grover Cleveland's administration, Davis served as a U.S. pension agent based in Philadelphia. Davis became a remarkable historian, documenting Bucks County's extensive history. He not only founded the Bucks County Historical Society but also wrote multiple books on local genealogy and history, including the popular read *The History of Bucks County, Pennsylvania*. Davis would later manage and edit the *Doylestown Democrat*, a small, politically partisan newspaper, in which he wrote about historical happenings in and around the area. Among other military and historical organizations, Davis also served as president of the American Historical Society, the Aztec Club, Society of Foreign Wars and the Society of the Army of the Potomac. Davis died in Doylestown on December 26, 1910, leaving behind him a multitude of historical research he compiled over the years he spent living in Bucks County.

IO

JAMES A. MICHENER

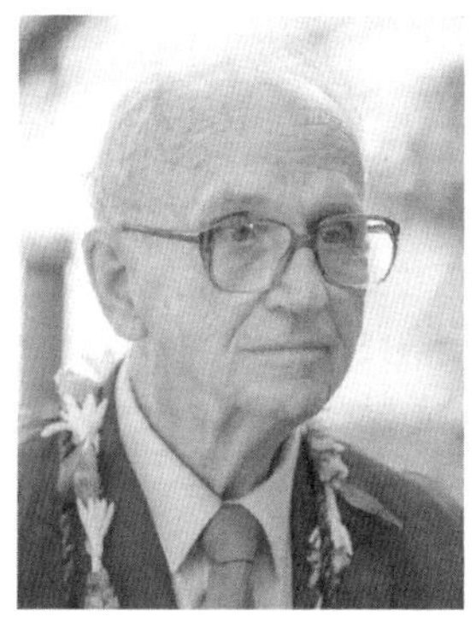

James A. Michener. *United States Federal Government.*

Another Doylestown resident, James A. Michener, became one of America's most beloved novelists and philanthropists. Raised a Quaker in Doylestown by his adoptive mother, Mabel, Michener said he never knew who his biological parents were or where exactly he was born. Some speculate that he was born on or about February 3, 1907. Despite the uncertainty about the date and place of his birth, James would eventually become a teacher, editor and naval historian in the South Pacific, known for his novels and short stories reflecting on foreign environments and fictional documentaries.

In 1925, James Michener graduated from Doylestown High School and attended Swarthmore College in Swarthmore, Pennsylvania, graduating summa cum laude four years later. Earning a bachelor of arts degree in English and history, Michener would later travel to Scotland and reside there for two years. Upon his return, he became a high school English teacher in Pottstown, Pennsylvania, and at the George School in Newtown, Bucks County. Several years later, Michener became a lieutenant in the U.S. Navy during World War II, motivating him to begin his writing career as a naval historian. By turning his notes and experiences into stories, such as his first book, the *Tales*

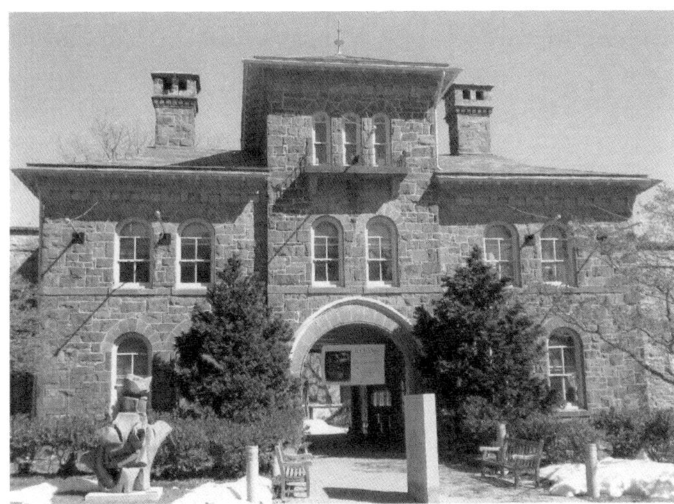

James A. Michener Art Museum, Doylestown, Bucks County.

of the South Pacific, winner of the Pulitzer Prize, Michener became a one-of-a-kind author and had numerous bestsellers.

Before his death on October 16, 1997, James A. Michener became an incredibly generous philanthropist, donating over $100 million to cultural and educational museums and institutions, including alma mater Swarthmore College and the James A. Michener Art Museum in Doylestown.

PART II

The Delaware Division of the Pennsylvania Canal and the Construction of the Durham Furnace

We noticed, in a previous chapter, the prevalence of Asiatic cholera, at the Bucks County Alms House, July 1849. It prevailed with equal fatality at the Durham Furnace. Whitaker & Co. were then building a new furnace and employed many hands. It was brought there by a man sick with it on a canal boat. The attention of the lock tender, Huff or Hough, was called to him. He looked in at him and then went away, but was taken sick in a few days and died. His family escaped. Samuel F. Hartman sat up with Hough; he also escaped, but his son, a child of nineteen months, took it and died.…In one instance, a whole family died with the exception of two children.
—William W.H. Davis

In 1827, the Pennsylvania legislature approved its plan to construct the Delaware Division of the Pennsylvania Canal as part of the development of a statewide system of canals. Pennsylvania was inspired by New York State's hugely successful Erie Canal, witnessing how the use of the canal system greatly improved the state's transportation. Soon thereafter, Pennsylvania began building a 1,200-mile canal system in order to connect Philadelphia, Pittsburgh and Lake Erie. These routes would allow for faster transportation of raw materials and manufacturing products, powering the nation's Industrial Revolution. According to the Friends of the Delaware Canal, a nonprofit organization in New Hope, one of the primary purposes of this waterway was to transport anthracite coal, usually found in areas surrounding valleys or mountains, from northeastern Pennsylvania to the cities along the East Coast of the United States.

II

IRISH LABORERS

The sixty-mile-long Delaware Division of the Pennsylvania Canal was completed in 1832, running from Bristol to Easton, connecting with the Lehigh Canal. Prior to the Civil War, mule-drawn boats traveled the route, moving approximately one million tons of coal per year. Other goods such as stone, lime, lumber and produce were transported. One of these boats could be loaded with eighty tons of cargo and was capable of traveling thirty miles or more per day. Men, women and children worked on the canals for over ten to twelve hours daily, with most shifts ending at or after ten o'clock at night.

All great things come with great sacrifice, and unfortunately, thousands of Irish immigrants sent to work on the canal experienced some of the worst atrocities Bucks County and the surrounding areas along the Delaware ever witnessed. Construction of the Delaware Division began in 1829 and was accomplished by Irish and German laborers, with the majority being Irish, using picks, shovels and wheelbarrows. Approximately three thousand Irishmen and women were brought to work on the canal by contractors from New York, a popular city for many emigrating from the Emerald Isle. The laborers were paid just forty to seventy cents per day for working sunrise to sunset, six days per week, regardless of the time spent on the canal. Skilled workers and laborers were called upon to build locks, bridges and buildings needed for the canal—these men were usually paid twenty-five cents more, or about a dollar per day. Work conditions were atrocious—many of the laborers were forced to live in crowded, unsanitary tents with little or barely edible food. Between 1832 and 1833, a cholera outbreak spread like wildfire through the camps along the canal, sickening hundreds of workers and their families, many dying from this horrific disease. Since conditions were so poor, many of the deceased were buried in unmarked graves along the canal—some since discovered, others still waiting to be found. Many workers also died in the construction of the railroad, as confirmed by a mass grave recently discovered at Duffy's Cut in Chester County.

12

THE DURHAM FURNACE

However, not all of the Irish immigrants in the area were employed on the canal or railroads. In 1727, three prominent Philadelphia merchants—William Allen, Joseph Galloway and James Logan—invested in the construction of a furnace and three forges along Durham Creek on what is now Durham Road. Durham Furnace would produce large amounts of bar iron, tools, pots, ornaments, fireplace equipment and iron for the next thirty years. The "Adam and Eve" stove, one that is similar to the famous Franklin Stove, was produced in mass quantities at the furnace from 1741 onward.

George Taylor, who emigrated from Ireland as an indentured servant and worked at the Warwick Furnace, formed a partnership to lease Durham Furnace in 1753, eventually producing an even greater variety of iron products. By the 1770s, George Taylor had become so involved with local politics as a member of the Pennsylvania Assembly that he organized militia companies in Bucks County and signed the Declaration of Independence.

By mixing his business and political interests, Taylor was able to transform the ironworks into a munitions factory for the Continental Army, producing cannons, cannonballs and other military equipment. His commitment to an independent United States was near and dear to his heart. Other workers at Durham Furnace were patriots, including Daniel Morgan, a general in the Continental Army. Durham Furnace's contributions to the Revolution were incredibly crucial to the cause, designing the famous "Durham Boat" in order to transport iron ore, charcoal and other goods along the canal

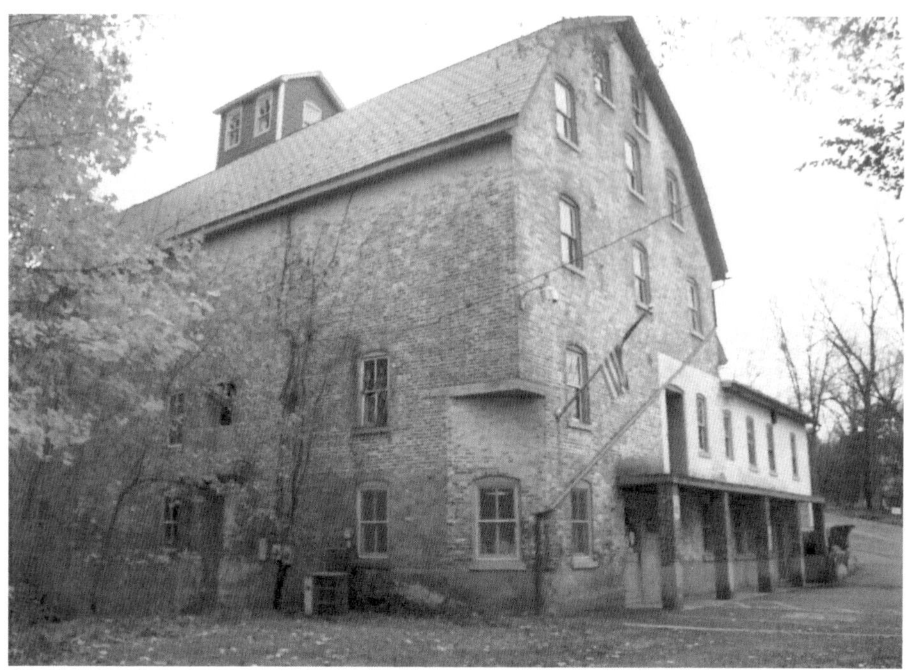

The Durham Furnace and Mill, Durham Township, Bucks County. Built 1727. One of the original managers was Colonel George Taylor, signer of the Declaration of Independence.

and Delaware River—many were used by the Continental Army during the winter of 1776. General George Washington and his army of 2,400 boarded these boats for their significant crossing of the Delaware River in December 1776.

The prevalence of cholera at the Durham Furnace, as well as the number of fatalities associated with the illness, was similar to what the laborers experienced on the Delaware Canal. According to William W.H. Davis, cholera was brought to the furnace by a man who arrived via a canal boat. The Irish who arrived to work at the furnace were the first victims. There were no religious services provided for the deceased, and the bodies were reportedly buried in trenches at the Haycock Catholic cemetery. Many women tended to the sick and prepared the dead for burial.

The ironworks owners made significant improvements to the factory throughout the 1800s, including the construction of a brick warehouse and a three-story stone gristmill on the site in 1820. Operating for over 150 years, the mill drew its water from nearby Cook's Creek.

The iron ore used at the Durham Furnace was found in the Durham hills. Limestone was also relatively easy to come by, as the famous Durham Caves were located just a short distance from the industrial site. The caves form a triangle at U.S. Route 611 and PA Route 212 and reportedly contained a "spring of excellent water," with the first of two caves running for approximately ninety yards. Archaeologists have discovered flint arrowheads, human skeletal remains, stone tools and various extinct animal fossils deep within. The first cave led to the second through a room that consisted of mineral deposits. The caves originally consisted of three rooms but were reduced to one due to quarrying during the nineteenth century.

PART III

Abolition and the Underground Railroad in Bucks County

We are Pennsylvanians, and we hope to see the day when Pennsylvania will have reason to be proud of us, as we believe she has now none to be ashamed. Will you starve our patriotism? Will you cast our hearts out of the treasury of the Commonwealth? Do you count our enmity better than our friendship?
—Appeal of Forty Thousand Citizens Threatened with Disfranchisement, to the People of Pennsylvania, *Robert Purvis, 1838*

Bucks County became incredibly significant to runaway slaves for its role in the Underground Railroad during the early to mid-nineteenth century. With numerous secret safe houses still unknown to many residents and visitors, fleeing slaves would often travel along the Delaware River on barges, making their way from Philadelphia to Bucks, New Jersey and finally New York City, allowing the slaves an easier escape to Canada. Several safe houses along the Delaware would welcome slaves and their families as part of the Underground Railroad, many offering safety, security and food as the freedom seekers made their journey north to Canada. Because of the state's overwhelming opposition to slavery and its premier geographic position as a border state between New Jersey and New York, Pennsylvania played a major role in the Underground Railroad. Bucks County also had abolitionist residents, particularly Quakers, who often fought for the rights of African Americans through a series of small, individual actions, assisting the fugitive slaves in obtaining freedom. Most of the safe houses in Bucks County were operated in properties owned by Quakers—many set up small spaces in the basements of their homes or businesses and used connecting tunnels to avoid confrontation from the community, as it was a federal crime to harbor and help fugitive slaves. However, some families, like the Magills, were alienated by the Quaker community for their involvement in active abolitionism. The number of Quakers in the county grew rapidly between 1679—the year the first village, called Crewcorne, now Morrisville, was founded by nearly a dozen Quaker families—and 1683, the establishment of the first Quaker meeting in Falls, Bucks County.

Compared to Chester and Philadelphia Counties, Bucks County's safe houses and stations were generally unorganized, set up quietly and then advertised by subtle word-of-mouth, some only identifiable by candlelight in a window. This branch of the Underground Railroad passed through the county as a narrow route, starting from Bristol, passing through Langhorne, Newtown, Buckingham and New Hope, to where the railroad "passengers" were transferred to another line. The Quaker community, particularly in Newtown, became the slaves' first stop for shelter before their next push to Yardley or New Hope, receiving help from several "conductors," such as Mahlon Linton. Linton, founder of the Pennsylvania Anti-Slavery Society and vice president of the Bucks County Anti-Slavery Society, was an active abolitionist and conductor of the Underground Railroad in the area. According to several reports, abolitionists Lucretia Mott, as well as Frederick Douglass, took the stage to engage audiences in the antislavery movement at Newtown Hall, or what is now Newtown Theatre.

Along their journey, runaway slaves would create codes, passwords and handshakes to help direct others in the right direction. An article written by Bucks County Quaker Dr. Edward Hicks Magill, former president of Swarthmore College, expressed how the county served an integral part of the Underground Railroad:

> [Bucks County] *is vividly described as having made up of a circle of Quaker residences enclosing a swampy place that swarmed with blacks. One may surmise that it made a model station. Slaves were transported at night across the Delaware River from the vicinity of Dover, in boats marked by a yellow light hung below a blue one, and were met some distance out from the Jersey shore by boats showing the same lights.... [T]hey were taken to Mount Holly, and so into the northern or Philadelphia route. Still, another branch of this Philadelphia line is known. It constitutes the fourth road, and is described by Mr. Robert Purvis as an extension of a route through Bucks County, Pennsylvania, that entered New Jersey, from Newtown, and ran directly to New Brunswick, then New York.*
> —*"When Men Were Sold, The Underground Railroad in Bucks County,"* published in the Friends' Intelligencer, *February 26, 1898*

13

The Purvis Brothers

Robert Purvis, founder of the Anti-Slavery Society of Philadelphia and sometimes referred to as the president of the Underground Railroad, was a well-known African American abolitionist in Bucks County. Both he and his brother Joseph, both of African descent, would transport slaves to the Bensalem area following Robert's purchase of land in what is now the Wellington Estates housing development.

Prior to moving to Bucks County, the Purvis brothers became well known in South Carolina, growing up as sons of an established cotton broker. The two worked diligently in their mission to secretly transport slaves, so much so that local historical societies were unaware of their involvement in the Underground Railroad until recently. In 1831, Robert Purvis purchased a large plot of land in Bensalem, naming it "The Grove." Just a few years later, Joseph moved into the area and acquired over two hundred acres of land previously known as the Eddington Farm. Despite Robert moving away from Bensalem, he still retained his strong ties to the township.

In 1831, Robert married Harriet Forten, daughter of James Forten, an African American businessman and abolitionist in Philadelphia. Robert began working with the Philadelphia Vigilance Committee, sheltering runaway slaves on the Underground Railroad. Two years later, Robert helped to establish the Library Company of Colored People, which assisted in the abolitionist movement. Traveling to Europe to speak publicly on the dangers and horrors of slavery, Robert would also raise funds and engage in meetings with high-ranking officials in the campaign to end slavery from around the world. In his effort, Robert drafted "Appeal of Forty Thousand Citizens Threatened with Disfranchisement" in 1838 to assist in his fight for abolition.

Records show that Robert continually utilized Joseph's property as a transfer station for slaves on the Underground Railroad. The two made an enormous impact on the movement in Bucks County, transferring slaves from Bristol and areas along the Delaware River to upper Bucks County—New Hope, Buckingham and Quakertown. Robert remained incredibly involved in the abolition of slavery alongside Quaker and antislavery and women's rights advocate Lucretia Mott. Together with Lucretia's husband, James, they assisted runaway fugitive slaves who fled Maryland and Delaware into Pennsylvania throughout the mid-nineteenth century.

Before Joseph's death in 1857 and Robert's in 1898, it is estimated that the Purvis brothers helped several thousand slaves escape slavery through their own estates. Both residences became known as safe houses. Their political efforts were directed toward abolitionism, women's rights, prison reform and prohibition.

14

HARRIET TUBMAN

Harriet Tubman, a renowned African American abolitionist, humanitarian and spy during the Civil War, was one of the leading black figures and organizers of the Underground Railroad, assisting over three hundred slaves escape from southern states to the "Promise Land." Born into slavery in Maryland in 1820, Tubman experienced the harsh brutality of a field hand, from beatings to lashings. Tubman's birth name was Araminta Ross but she later changed her name after marrying John Tubman, a free African American, and adopted her mother's name, Harriet.

After escaping slavery and leaving her husband and family behind in Maryland in 1849, Harriet Tubman moved to Philadelphia, where she pioneered the Underground Railroad movement with the help of prominent abolitionists already stationed in and around the city. Following her journey to Philadelphia, Tubman founded the Underground Railroad of Bucks County by traveling along certain routes, establishing contacts along the Delaware and other areas throughout the county. Some of these safe houses were likely located by Tubman during her many travels from the South to the North, highlighting sites and pathways many other documented Underground Railroad passengers traveled. While it is difficult to determine how much of an impact Harriet Tubman made directly in Bucks County, it is well known that she brought dozens of fleeing slaves from the southern states through Pennsylvania along the Delaware, perhaps establishing the safe houses that hundreds more journeyed to in the years to follow.

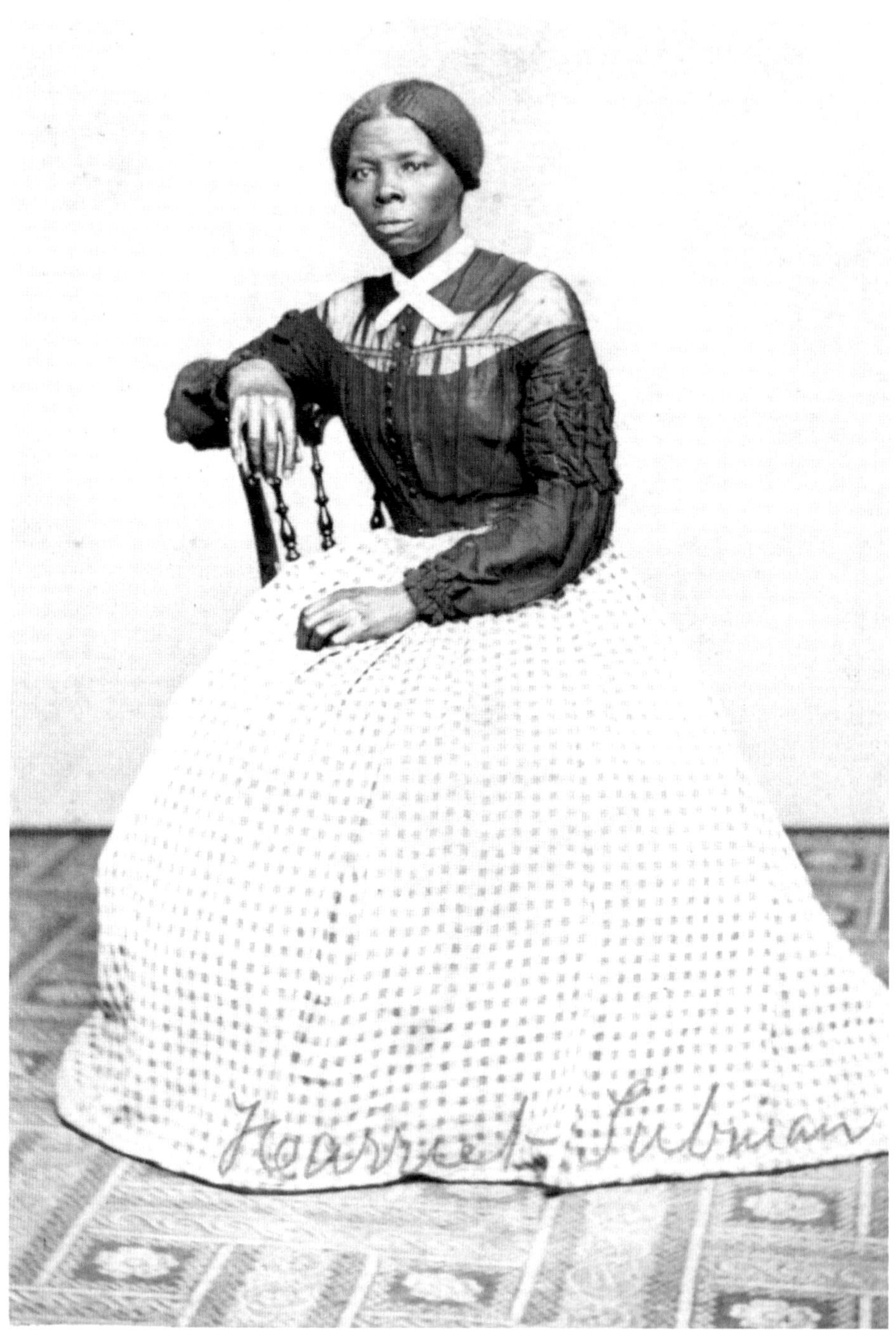

Portrait of Harriet Tubman by Benjamin Powelson, 1868. *Library of Congress, Prints and Photographs Division.*

Throughout her first few years as a conductor on the Underground Railroad, Tubman returned to Maryland to rescue her family, friends and other slaves one group at a time, guiding dozens, and some say hundreds, to freedom, never losing sight of a single "passenger." Following the Fugitive Slave Act of 1850, Harriet Tubman continued her efforts in transporting and guiding slaves even farther north into Pennsylvania, New York and New England, helping the newly freed slaves find work and a happier life.

Located in Lions Park in Bristol is a magnificent statue of the abolitionist. The statue, depicting Harriet Tubman pointing toward the North Star, is molded from solid bronze and stands approximately six feet tall. The statue is one of three of Tubman in the country—Boston, Ohio and Bristol.

15

Local Stops along the Underground Railroad

During the later years of the slavery agitation a branch of the "underground railroad," a mythical corporation to help runaway slaves toward the North Pole, passed through Bucks County. It was "narrow gauge," and starting from Bristol ran up through the county via Attleborough, Newtown, Buckingham to New Hope, where the through passengers were transferred to another line.
—William W.H. Davis

The Underground Railroad was kept secret, as were the stations and conductors operating within the movement. However, in Bucks County, there are quite a few well-known taverns, bed-and-breakfasts and residences that once served a monumental role in the Underground Railroad, some of which are still standing today. Unfortunately, due to lack of evidence from personal accounts, some of these stations are only speculated to have been part of the Underground Railroad. However, many of these structures had tunnels leading runaway slaves to their next stop on the course to freedom.

WARMINSTER

The final route of the Northeastern Corridor ran from Norristown to the Hatboro-Horsham area (Montgomery County), ending in New Hope. Old York Road proceeded from Philadelphia to the Hatboro-Horsham

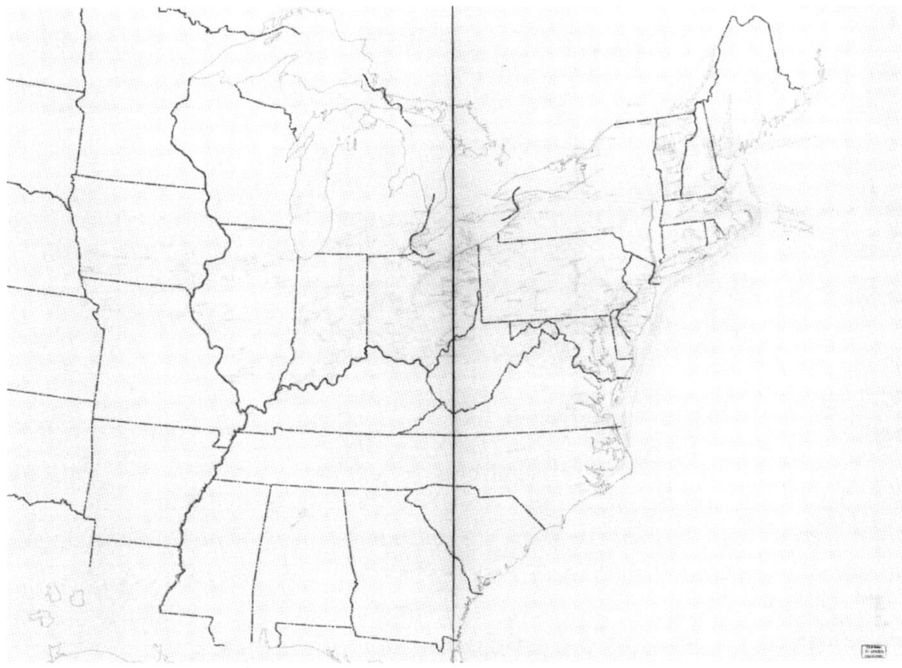

Underground Railroad map of the United States, circa 1838–60. *Library of Congress, Geography and Map Division.*

area and continued through Warminster Township and Doylestown. Both towns were rumored to have had Underground Railroad stations. Being that there were many Quakers in and around these towns, it is probable that some of the meetinghouses or residences could have been stations for the Underground Railroad.

The Warminster Meeting House was established by Horsham Meeting in 1840. Since Quaker Friends living in Warminster had to travel nearly five miles to Horsham for worship, Quaker Thomas Parry, originally of Caernarvonshire, Wales (b. 1680), purchased an acre of land and built a meetinghouse that was fifty-four feet long by twenty-seven feet wide. The total cost of the meetinghouse and enclosed burial ground was $1,400. It was approved as a preparative meeting in June 1841. The Friends of the Warminster Meeting were very active in humanitarian efforts, including collecting aid and sewing uniforms for Union soldiers during the Civil War. According to William W.H. Davis, Thomas Parry was a reputed abolitionist in Bucks County, though his involvement with the Underground Railroad is unknown.

NEW HOPE

Located on 111 West Bridge Street in New Hope is a beautifully preserved historic bed-and-breakfast called the Wedgwood Inn. The elegant structure was built in or around 1870 by Maryann Slaughter on the foundation of the "Old Fort," General Alexander's (also known as Lord Stirling) headquarters two weeks prior to the Battle of Trenton in 1776. General William Alexander was one of George Washington's military generals during the American Revolution. Alexander held many ranks throughout his life, including as a supply officer during the French and Indian War, as well as brigadier general in 1776. Just one year later, he took part in the Battles of Brandywine and Germantown, while also playing a key role in the exposure of a conspiracy by Thomas Conway to unseat General Washington. It is said that General Washington, alongside Generals Knox, Sullivan, Greene and Alexander, laid plans for the Battle of Trenton opposite the Old Fort. Approximately 1,200 troops were stationed across the street from what is now the Wedgwood Inn.

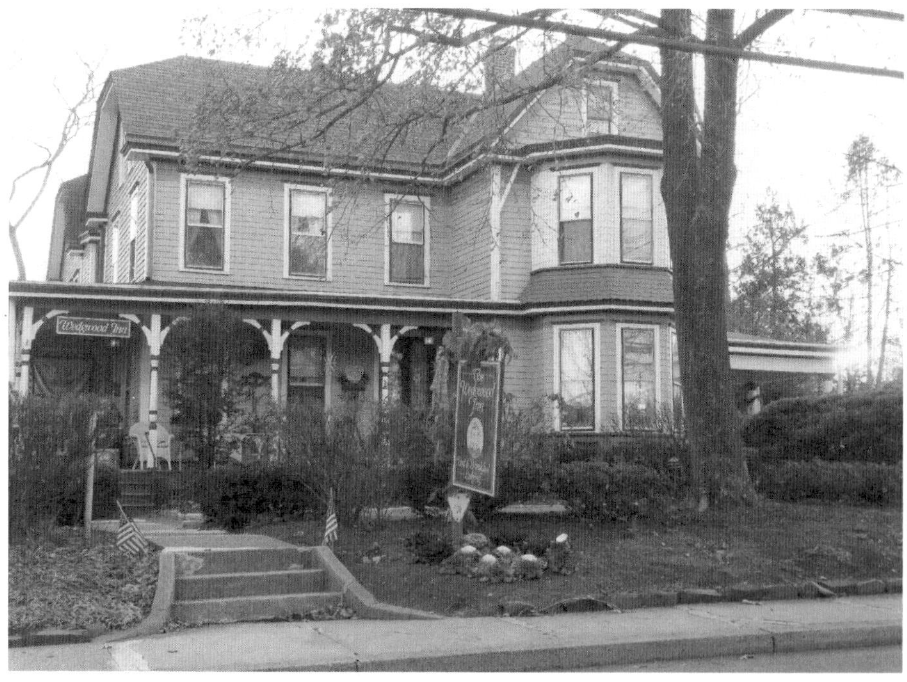

Wedgwood Inn, New Hope, Bucks County. The bed-and-breakfast may have once housed many runaway slaves as part of the Underground Railroad.

Then an old hip roof house, the site would later welcome runaway slaves traveling along the Underground Railroad.

In 1990, when the Wedgwood was renovated, a tunnel was uncovered, either indicating a prior life as a Continental Army ammunitions storage facility or a station of the Underground Railroad. During this renovation, the remains of a Hessian soldier were found hidden within the chimney of a fireplace in the basement. This exact same tunnel may have also been used as a station of the Underground Railroad, perhaps an important stop leading the runaway slaves from Bensalem to Quakertown. Legend has it that the spirit of a twelve-year-old former slave tries to tell the story of how she escaped slavery to younger guests who visit the Wedgwood Inn.

YARDLEY

In the center of Yardley sits one of the oldest surviving taverns in Bucks County: the Continental Tavern. In 1860, Samuel Slack was granted a license to establish a restaurant in the same building where he had operated an "unlicensed tavern," or temperance house, store and town library, permitting the sale of "intoxicating liquors." The original tavern license was witnessed by John Yardley, a descendant of the borough's founding family, and signed by Samuel Slack and Joseph Moon. Samuel's tavern and boardinghouse was called the Yardleyville Hotel. In 1866, when the tavern received the name the Continental Hotel, the license was transferred to Aaron Slack. The stone foundation of the tavern itself dates back to the American Revolution as an original building of the Yardley estate. In 1876, a fire destroyed the property, and in 1877, it was rebuilt.

In 2007, the property was purchased by the Lyons and Vliet families, who had dreams of restoring the property as it was during the nineteenth century. During restoration and an archaeological excavation of the property, owner Frank Lyons and his team discovered a set of stone walls below the kitchen in the basement. After a few hours of digging approximately twenty-five feet deep, they discovered three hidden chambers measuring fifteen by fifteen feet long with eighteen-inch stone walls. According to the proprietors, there is a good chance that the Continental Tavern led the fugitive slaves to a nearby gristmill, the Lake Afton historic house or Lake Side, being that all three are in proximity to one other. The basement of the tavern contains chambers that were likely used to hide the runaway slaves as they fled the South. While searching for evidence of the Underground

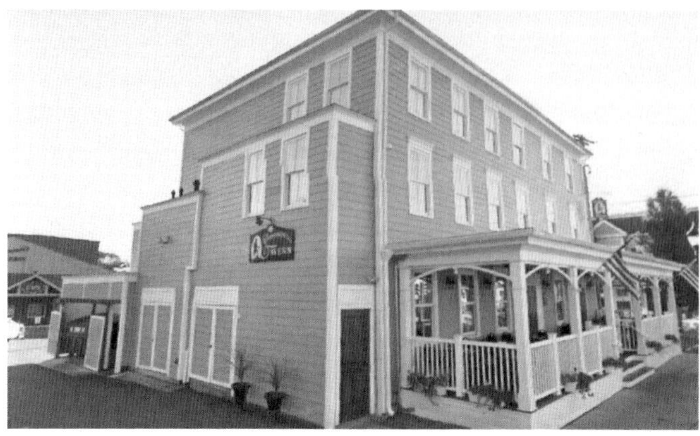

The Continental Tavern, Yardley, Bucks County. The historic tavern played a role as a station along the Underground Railroad.

Railroad, the team of excavators discovered over ten thousand empty whiskey bottles from the Prohibition era, coins, apothecary and personal care items, automobile parts and a "mysterious weapon" hidden alongside a woman's blood-ridden corset. Perhaps this evidence signifies that not only did the property welcome fleeing slaves but also played an immense role in Prohibition in Bucks County, perhaps as a speakeasy.

With one of the oldest Quaker meetings in Pennsylvania being in Yardley, it would be of no surprise that the Quakers living in the town would assist the slaves in seeking shelter. Yardley is perfectly situated between Newtown, a largely Quaker town at the time, as well as New Hope, another town with known safe houses, so it is possible that the tunnel below the Continental Tavern connected to an even larger tunnel system. After further excavation, it is believed that the tunnel extends at least two to three stories below the property.

Telford

Located in Telford, Upper Bucks County, the Rising Sun Inn, known previously as Gerhart's Tavern, has witnessed significant moments in history. The Rising Sun Inn was once a station along the Underground Railroad for many slaves seeking refuge in the northern states, some sent by abolitionist Seth Lukens of Lansdale, Montgomery County, and others by conductor Richard Moore of Quakertown.

Built in 1739 by George Esterly, the property was leased to Peter and Elizabeth Gerhart in 1752. Gerhart's became an overnight stop for stagecoaches traveling from Philadelphia to Allentown.

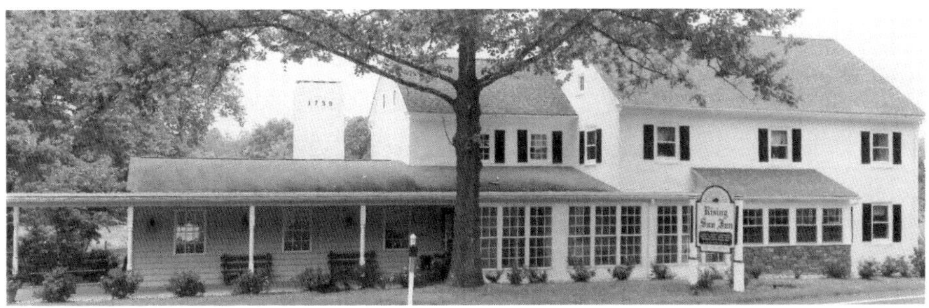

Rising Sun Inn. Telford, Bucks County. Built in 1739, opened as Gerhart's Tavern in 1752 by Peter and Elizabeth Gerhart, the inn housed runaway slaves as part of the Underground Railroad.

For the runaway slaves, traveling through northeastern Pennsylvania to New York was exhaustive, as there were sometimes more than ten miles between stations. The "Bucks County Line" extended to Quakertown—a major depot on the Underground Railroad. One of the earliest known maps of the Underground Railroad trail shows a line between Norristown and Quakertown, stretching approximately twenty-five miles long. The escape line was not likely to have been completed in one night, so it is speculated that there were a number of resting stations between the two towns, dividing the route so that the slaves could seek shelter along the way. To reach Quakertown from Norristown, the runaways traveled along Dekalb Pike (or Route 202) until they reached the Old Bethlehem Pike outside of Lansdale. Dr. Paxton, an honorable abolitionist and conductor, would sometimes transfer hundreds of the slaves to Quakertown through the means of Seth Lukens of Lansdale. The runaway slaves would travel eight more miles following their departure from Lukens's home to Gerhart's Tavern on Allentown Road. The Gerharts welcomed the fugitives overnight in the tunnels that had been dug out in the basement to replenish and refuel prior to continuing their journey north.

According to the Rising Sun Inn's website, the Liberty Bell was housed overnight in Gerhart's Tavern in order to avoid it being captured by the British during their occupation of Philadelphia in 1777.

NORTHAMPTON TOWNSHIP

Founded on December 14, 1722, and covering over twenty miles, Northampton Township is believed to have received its name from the county of Northampton in the English midlands, approximately one hundred miles north of London. By the mid-nineteenth century, the township consisted of five villages: Richboro, Addisville, Churchville, Rocksville and Jacksonville. Today, Addisville is Richboro, Rocksville is Holland and Jacksonville is Ivyland.

A section of the Bennett Search House, a small farmhouse that has been standing for over three hundred years in Richboro, was built in approximately 1731 and has been home to several Bucks County families. The home has significant history hidden beneath the floorboards.

In the late 1600s, the Bennett family moved to Northampton Township from Holland; Abraham Bennett purchased several acres of land in 1687. About forty years later, Abraham's cousin William bought the land on which the Bennett Search House, also referred to as Hampton Hill, stands, building the first section of the house shortly thereafter. For over four decades, William, a blacksmith, his wife, Charity, and their ten children resided in the historic home. The Bennetts are believed to be the earliest immigrants from Holland to settle in the township. The house was owned by the Bennetts during the nineteenth century, followed by the Search family—Bennett descendants.

According to the Northampton Historical Society, the historic farmhouse has a unique past, including several legends that are, of course, up to interpretation. However, one claim, that the house harbored slaves on the Underground Railroad, is thought to have the most evidence. During restoration, an old stone archway to one of the cellars was found, supporting the legend that the house may have been used as a station for slaves on the Underground Railroad. There are also rumors that a slave burial ground is located approximately two hundred yards north of the house, but there are no known records to confirm this claim.

16

RUNAWAY SLAVES OF BUCKS COUNTY

Hundreds of former slaves set foot in Bucks County throughout the mid-nineteenth century; however, while some figures are based on the assumption that fleeing slaves had to travel through the county and along the Delaware to further their journey, others are proven with the help of Dr. Edward Hicks Magill. Magill, a birthright Quaker and former president of Swarthmore College, wrote a paper, later published in 1909, on the Underground Railroad in Bucks County. Jonathan Magill, Edward's father and Quaker teacher, owned a farm along the edge of Solebury Mountain, a popular stop along the Underground Railroad for many fleeing slaves. Jonathan was involved in the American Anti-Slavery Society, and with his sons, Edward and Watson, joined the Underground Railroad. Many of these men and women told Edward and his family the stories of their lives as slaves, including stops in Lower Bucks County—where they first journeyed to following their departure from Philadelphia—and Central Bucks County, with many safe houses provided by the Atkinson, Trego, Smith, Simpson, Paxon, Magill and Fell families. Sometimes, the fleeing families would move on to Quakertown or Canada. With the help of a "black handyman," Jonathan and his sons received passengers from other conductors in Norristown, passing them onto William Henry Johnson in Philadelphia or Richard and Sarah Moore in Quakertown.

In 1845, Dr. Edward H. Magill, also a teacher in Langhorne, maintained his family's tradition as an abolitionist. He assisted at least six runaway slaves who traveled along the Delaware River from Maryland. Dressed as a farmer heading to New Jersey via ferry, Edward covered the men with a tarp and completed a thirty-mile journey, avoiding detection by slave catchers.

Rachel Moore of Elkton, Maryland, traveled through several safe houses with her six children prior to arriving in Bucks County. Rachel and her family stumbled across the Magill property wearing just dirty, tattered rags. The Magills allowed Rachel and her children to remain at the household for several years.

> [Rachel Moore] *was manumitted by her master, and received free-papers from the court at Elkton. I had hoped to present these papers, as they were long carefully cherished in her possession, but they have been mislaid since her death. She had six children who were still slaves, and succeeded in bringing all of them North, aided by the Underground Railroad. As usual they traveled only by night, resting in concealment during the day. Think of a mother starting unaided, with her six children, to a distant and unknown country, seeking for her children the blessings of freedom which she herself had already acquired! Does the fact speak volumes for the cruelty of a system of oppression from which she was making her escape? They sometimes met with friends who took them in and cared for them at night. Sometimes they were less fortunate, and spent the day of anxious concealment all alone. The first names that I have of those with whom they stopped are a family of Lewises with whom they spent two days at Phoenixville, and who then sent them on, in a wagon at night, to a friend named Paxon near Norristown, who in turn took them into Norristown to the home of that well-known friend of the slave, Jacob L. Paxon, where they remained two weeks. From there they were forwarded to the home of W.H. Johnson, where homes were found for the four eldest children in the families of Thomas Paxon, Joseph Fell, Edward Williams and John Blackfan. Rachel, with her two younger children, came to the home of my father, Jonathan P. Magill, where they remained for several years.*
> —*"When Men Were Sold, The Underground Railroad in Bucks County," Jonathan P. Magill,* Friends' Intelligencer, *1898*

Richard Moore, a well-known Underground Railroad stationmaster, arrived in Quakertown in 1813. By 1830, escaped slaves could seek refuge and assistance at Moore's Penrose Pottery on South Main Street. By the Civil War, it is said that over six hundred escaped slaves had passed through the station on their journey to freedom. By the time the refugees reached these northern points, many would have already traveled miles hungry and desperate. Numerous Underground Railroad conductors would forward the slaves to Moore, knowing that his station was the last and final stop in Bucks County—the point where northern Chester County and Bucks County converged.

Between 1813 and 1825, Moore, a teacher at that time, achieved a favorable reputation as a model citizen. In 1819, Richard married prominent Quaker Sarah Foulke, whose father was a member of the Pennsylvania General Assembly, and they had two children, John Jackson and Hannah. During this time, Richard needed a steadier and more profitable occupation, prompting him to purchase a pottery originally founded by Able Penrose along Bethlehem Pike in Quakertown. Moore had his home constructed next to the pottery in 1834, and by 1850, his pottery had become one of the largest employers in Richland Township. Richard and his wife, Sarah, decided to join the Underground Railroad system just a few years later, making them another Bucks County Quaker family to assist in the movement. Richard Moore's home and pottery became known as the northernmost stop in Bucks County. Escaped passengers would come from other stations in Lower Bucks County or Norristown, Montgomery County. When safe, the fleeing refugees would be moved to another northern station.

From his grandson, Alfred Moore, of Philadelphia, I learn that Richard Moore, while not ready to unite with the early abolitionists in their revolutionary motto: No Union with Slaveholders, still felt prompted by sympathy many years ago to aid on their way the escaping fugitives. His home soon became known to friends further South as a place where all fugitives forwarded would receive care and needed assistance in their continued flight. Thence they soon began to come directed to his home in very considerable numbers. Although slaveholders rarely proceeded so far in pursuit of their slaves, they occasionally did so, and more than once the master has presented himself at the front door of Richard Moore a few moments after the object of his search, being forewarned of his approach, had escaped by a back door to a place of concealment in the rear. Many of the fugitives, on reaching Quakertown, feeling comparatively safe, were willing to hire out there, and Richard Moore was ever willing to give them work himself, or find them employment among his friends and neighbors.
—"When Men Were Sold, The Underground Railroad in Bucks County,"
the Friends' Intelligencer, *1898*

BENJAMIN JONES

The most notable refugee who entered Bucks County via the Underground Railroad was Reverend Benjamin Jones, a former slave from Little York, Maryland, who later coordinated his ministry with the rescue of runaway slaves. Also nicknamed "Big Ben" for his size, while enslaved, Jones ran from the auction block with four other men with the help of operatives of the Underground Railroad, assisting them in their journey to Buckingham Mountain. Jones would soon find work with Thomas Bye, Jonathan Fell and William Stavely, for whom he was employed for about eleven years.

In 1826, Reverend Jones continued his mission to preach and supervise the Underground Railroad from Mount Gilead African Methodist Episcopal Church in New Hope, Bucks County. According to Dr. Edward Magill, while chopping wood near Solebury, Jones was seized by his master, William Anderson, and four bounty hunters. Big Ben desperately defended himself with nothing but an axe, and despite having all of his assailants on the ground at one point, he was eventually overpowered and removed from the property without a hearing. Because of his injuries, Benjamin was unable to be sold. At a meeting held in Forestville, now Solebury, on May 26, 1844, the local Quakers raised funds to purchase Benjamin's freedom at the cost of $700. Unfortunately, due to his injuries, after working for just a short time, Benjamin and his wife, Sarah Johnson, of Norristown, spent his remaining days at the Bucks County Alms House, located on Route 611 in Doylestown, where he later passed away.

The neighborhood talk for a few days past has been concerning the capture of that giant of a runaway slave known by the cognomen of little Ben.

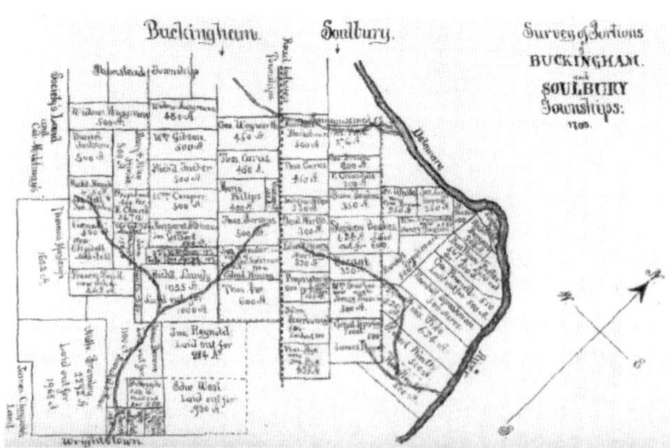

Survey map of Solebury and Buckingham Townships, 1795. *History of Bucks County, Pennsylvania.* William W.H. Davis.

He was chopping in the woods when he was accosted by three strangers (his master and another person remaining in the carriage out of sight) who told him that he must go with them. He refused and they fell on him. Ben fought like a hero came near cutting one fellow's head off with his axe but was at last so disabled by their clubs that he had to give up. That notorious character Squire Bailey is generally suspected of having given information of Ben. If guilty he ought certainly to feel the Negro's vengeance.
—letter dated March 23, 1844, from Richard [surname unknown] of Buckingham Township to Jacob F. Byrnes of Wilmington, Delaware

Mount Gilead Community Church

Mount Gilead Community Church, nestled along what is now Holicong Road atop Buckingham Mountain, is a small stone church beloved by local residents and historians. With just one room and a partial basement, Mount Gilead welcomed many of Benjamin Jones's sermons. Freed blacks and runaway slaves are said to have built log and stone cabins on the mountain, encouraged by local abolitionists and Quakers. While difficult to provide an accurate history of the Underground Railroad on this mountain, the sheltering of runaway slaves and the geography of the church itself may prove to be fact rather than fiction, especially with the rocky terrain and caves the mountain provided the refugees. After all, the Underground Railroad had to be carried out in secret. However, well-

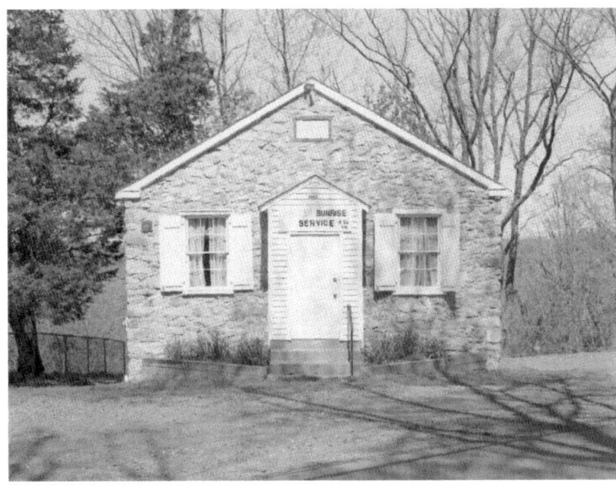

Mount Gilead AME Church, Holicong Road, New Hope, Bucks County. *Historic American Buildings Survey, Library of Congress.*

known Underground Railroad conductors and one of the most recognized abolitionist families of Bucks County, the Trego family, held a fundraiser on the church property in 1863.

In 1822, the congregation had fifteen families but no physical place of worship, forcing members to meet in their homes. Many of the earliest African Methodist Episcopal, or AME, histories refer to the congregation as the "Mountain." Just twelve years later, the congregation became large enough to begin construction of the structure, making it one of the oldest AME churches in Bucks County. In 1852, the congregation rebuilt the structure out of rose quartz and stones quarried from the mountain, making the church slightly larger, and covering the stones with stucco. By the end of the nineteenth century, many of the mountain's residents migrated to other towns such as Bristol, New Hope, Newtown, Solebury, Wrightstown and Doylestown, causing the congregation to dwindle.

Basil Dorsey

The case of Basil Dorsey, another slave from Maryland, but of Frederick County, is one of the most exciting for the fleeing slave, as well as recognized abolitionist Robert Purvis. In 1837, Basil Dorsey fled his master, Thomas E. Sollers, and was living with Robert Purvis of Bensalem.

Basil Dorsey and his three brothers fled from Plantation Liberty, Frederick County, on May 14, 1836. Originally named Ephraim Costly under master and assumed father Sabrick Sollers, Basil claimed that he and his brothers were promised their freedom upon their master's death. However, Sollers's son Thomas refused to honor his father's promise, prompting the brothers to escape and travel along the Underground Railroad, where they would find assistance from Robert Purvis. Thomas, the youngest of the brothers, decided to reside in Philadelphia, whereas Robert transported Charles, William and Basil to his and his brother's station in Bensalem, where they all adopted the surname Dorsey.

A few years later, the brothers were discovered, and former master Thomas Sollers enlisted a bounty hunter to reclaim his slaves. Thomas was captured in Philadelphia and taken to Baltimore, but a group of abolitionists raised money for his freedom. A warrant for the arrest of Basil, Charles and William was obtained from Judge Fox from Doylestown. Charles and William were able to escape Bucks County with the help of Joseph Purvis to a conductor in New Jersey. Basil Dorsey was overtaken and handcuffed, jailed in Bristol and then brought to Doylestown for his trial.

David Paul Brown, a prominent abolitionist lawyer from Philadelphia, was hired by Robert Purvis to defend Basil in the trial. Basil's former master, Thomas, offered to sell Basil to Purvis, but Basil immediately interjected, declaring that he would rather commit suicide than go back into slavery. Robert Purvis's recollections indicate that following the trial in Doylestown, he transported Basil Dorsey to his mother's house twenty-six miles from Philadelphia, later placing him in the hands of Underground Railroad conductor Joshua Leavitt of New York. Basil Dorsey was safely delivered to New England, where he lived out the rest of his life as a free man.

Before the hearing came on, the master had offered to accept one thousand dollars for his slave and the money could easily have been raised, but this Dorsey forbade his friends doing, saying "I am prepared to take my life it the case goes against me, for I will never to back to slavery." The case proceeded, and when partly through the question of Maryland being a slave state came up and on this the court ruled against the master. Time was asked for, but refused and the case was dismissed. The friends of Dorsey now hurried him away and the "Underground Railroad" soon carried him to a place of safety. Subsequently one hundred and fifty dollars were paid [to] the master to prevent future trouble. Dorsey passed the remainder of his life in Massachusetts and prospered.

—William W.H. Davis

PART IV

From Civil War to Dentistry: One Bucks County Soldier's Account and Life after the War

Between 1861 and 1865, the United States of America divided, bringing forth the Civil War. The war began when seven Southern states declared independence from the country and seceded, promoting slavery and becoming the Confederate States of America. A total of eleven states joined the Confederacy. The remaining states, the Union, supported the abolition of slavery. After nearly four years of a strictly American-soil battle, the Confederacy collapsed, slavery was abolished and the movement toward freedom and rights for all African Americans began. Thousands of Philadelphia-area soldiers, consisting of men from its surrounding counties, including Bucks, enlisted in the war effort.

Bucks County is rich in Civil War history, including the 104th Pennsylvania Volunteer Regiment under Colonel William W.H. Davis, a prominent figure in documenting the county's history. Camp Lacey, named for Brigadier General John Lacey of the American Revolutionary War, was established to train the militia in Doylestown. The camp was located at the site of what is now Central Bucks West High School. W.W.H. Davis, born in Southampton Township in July 1820, was given permission by the secretary of war to recruit a regiment and six-gun battery to join the war effort. Within ten days, Davis had over four hundred men enrolled.

Nearly 1,050 men left Doylestown to fight for the Union, including Father William Gries of St. Paul's Episcopal Church, who became the regiment's chaplain. Also called the Ringgold Regiment by Davis, the 104th Regiment departed to Washington, D.C., to join the Army of the Potomac in November 1861. Davis took the necessary precautions to protect his regiment from disease, including having them vaccinated for smallpox prior to entering the war.

However, not all Bucks County men enlisted in the 104th—some would enter the war effort through regiments based out of Philadelphia, including Private Joseph Lehman Eisenbrey of Lumberville, Bucks County. Though his time spent in the Civil War was shorter than others, being that he enlisted in Philadelphia on February 15, 1865, Eisenbrey's experiences were nothing short of interesting. Eisenbrey enlisted at the age of twenty-three as a private in the 8th Pennsylvania Cavalry, Company C, and was later promoted to company clerk.

Eisenbrey was born on March 18, 1842, in Lumberville to Henry E. Eisenbrey and Mary Ann Walker Eisenbrey. Henry, a Methodist minister in Lumberville, a town just several miles from the resort town of New Hope, once lived on a farm in Hatboro, Montgomery County, in 1835 alongside his brother, Peter. The two brothers became active in the Union Sunday School but soon after decided to organize the Methodists into a class meeting. Henry and Peter began preaching at their own Sunday school in a "little red, octagonal schoolhouse" formerly located at the corner of York Road and Monument Avenue, Hatboro.

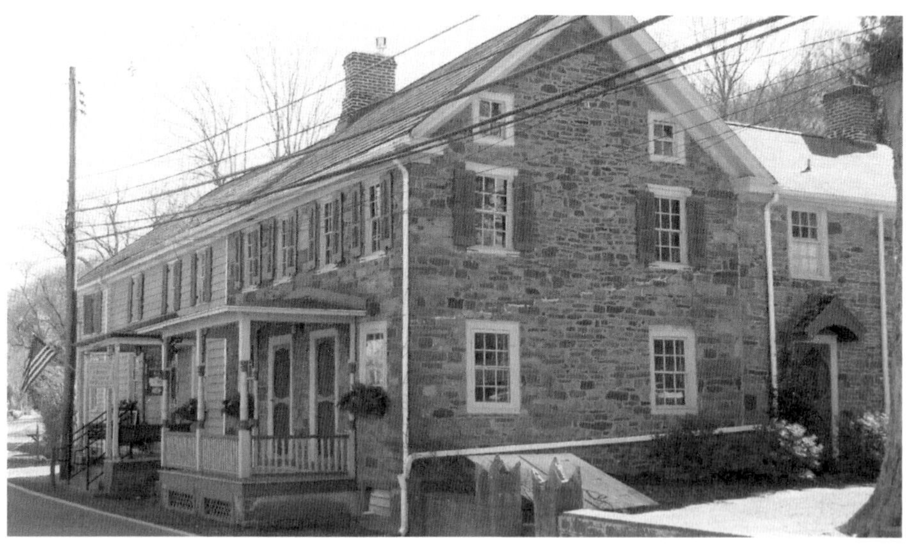

Lumberville General Store, Lumberville, Bucks County. Reportedly the oldest remaining general store in Pennsylvania.

More than 50 infantry and cavalry regiments were recruited in and around Philadelphia. In addition, 11 U.S. Colored Troops units were organized in Philadelphia. The state's call for volunteers was met with the enlistment of over 400,000 soldiers and fielded 270 regiments. Numerous training camps were formed throughout the state, including Camp Cadwalader in Philadelphia.

Prior to the Civil War, Joseph Lehman Eisebrey found himself a job as a carpenter's apprentice at the age of sixteen. Within the first few weeks of his enlistment, J.L. Eisenbrey was promoted from "High Private to Company Clerk." According to the *Dental Cosmos* volume 14, not only was Eisenbrey the dispatch-bearer of his regiment but he also "acted on different occasions as Lietuenent [*sic*]." As clerk, Joseph was able to continue writing his journals since he was in charge of the company's books, reports, payrolls and "in fact, all the writing of the company."

In the *Journal of Joseph Lehman Eisenbrey, A Civil War Diary*, located at the Spruance Library of the Mercer Museum, J.L. Eisenbrey wrote graphically of what he experienced while on the battlefield and at camp, from deceased bodies lying in fields to smoke-filled skies and flying cannonballs. Eisenbrey's vivid descriptions of the events he witnessed certainly depict what life was like fighting in the Civil War. Joseph dealt with similar hardships to the thousands of other soldiers on the battlefield. He survived the war despite the scarce food supplies, his rotten shoes and the cold, damp ground as bedding.

17

CIVIL WAR DIARY

Courtesy of the Spruance Library, Mercer Museum

Mar 7th, 65. I fried some hard tack and pork for breakfast. We have not much of a variety here. I saddled Frank and went over to have our photographs taken but they do not take them till 4 oclock. Our Cap't drilled us with the…exercise this fore noon. I liked it very much but it was very hard on my arms holding on to it so long and tight, and it being the first time. This afternoon we were drilled on horse back then I went over and had my photographs taken sitting on Frank with my arms in the position to make a left cut at infantry or cavalry. It is not a very good one it is all most a hassle to get one at all. I paid $2.00 for it. We drew rations…for 3 days and nights this evening. We are going on picket tomorrow morning at a place called Ald Chuck, about 5 miles from our camp. Our rations consisted of a chunk of fresh beef and pork, loaf of bread, hard tack, some beans and sugar and coffee. I also bought 5lb of potatoes at 10 [illegible] per pound. I boiled some for dinner. It was quite noisy here this morning from the Brigade firing off and clearing their fire arms. I have not shot off mine yet. I just loaded my pistol last night and received cartage for my carbine this evening. It has been another nice day. I washed 2 pairs of drawers, 1 undershirt, towel and handkerchief, it's the first washing I have done yet I used plenty of boiling water and soap and succeeded in getting them clean. They boys are gambling again this evening. I was put on horseguard this evening, the 3rd relief, from 3 to 6 morning. It will be the first time that I was ever on guard. I will soon be an old soldier.

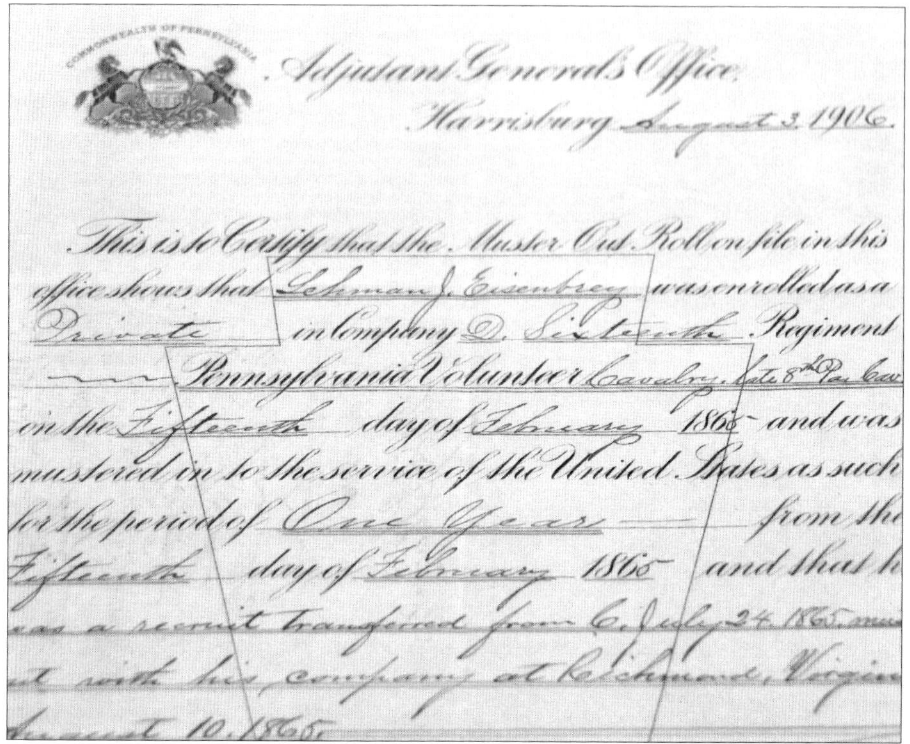

Joseph Lehman Eisenbrey, enrollment papers. Dated August 3, 1906. Spruance Library and Mercer Museum. *Courtesy of Penn State University, Abington.*

Thurs. Mar 16th, 1865. I am just 23 years old today and hope to live to see another birthday. I was just on garrison duty this morning at 10 for the first time and will come off tomorrow at 10 o'clock. My post was No 2 at Headquarters (before the officers Quarters). I had to walk my best all the time, it was 2 hours on and 4 off. If we are caught not walking our beat, the punishment is that we have to shoulder a log and carry it for 2 hours. We have to salute all officers that pass. It is hard work walking our beat continuously. It makes my back ache so that I can hardly stand at some times. It commenced to rain about 9 o'clock this eve and rained very hard, and blew a perfect hurricane. I was out in it till 10 on my post.

Sat. April 8th.
General Custer passed us again this morning with his "battle flags" fluttering in the wind. After he passed we started. We passed through

Prospect Ridge and Franklin, both small towns and mostly deserted. Just before night 5 trains of cars loaded with forage and provision fell into our hands…in the way, just as our men got to the station on the Lynchburg and Petersburg R.R. a telegraph dispatch was sent there to know if they (The Rebs.) wanted them sent down. So our men sent back word to send them on immediately, decidedly a good joke on them. Our boys have been out foraging today and some of them are quite lively, having found plenty of "apple jacks." We were each supplied with 100 rounds of ammunition and told that we would have occasion to use them soon. Every indication along the road goes to show that the two armies are coming in contact soon. It is surprising to see what an amount of wagons, caissons and property that we have destroyed for them.

April 9th, 1865. Sunday.
We double quicked it to the front, the fighting had been going on sometime and the jonnies were driving our boys back as they always do at first but soon reinforcements came up of both cavalry, artillery, and infantry (the 24th com. of Negroes) there the tide of the battle changed. Sheridan took his cavalry around to the left to flank them, there they had a heavy force of cavalry to meet us. They had skirmishers stationed around to pick us off our horses as we were forming in line to charge them. I must confess that I ducked my head once there for a peace commissioner came decidedly close and what made it worse was that we were not allowed to fire back then as we could not see them. (The 8th Reg't was front as usual) Soon the Bugle sounded, "Charge" then with a yell we started on the gallop. The Rebels could not resist long but broke and run. Although I cannot boast of killing a jonnie for certain or taking one prisoner, I can say without any boasting that I was the closer to the jonnies at the "Charge" than any member of my Reg't or Company and just escaped being captured. Soon after the bugle sounded the "charge" forward, it sounded "halt" but we paid no attention to it. An "orderly" had just been brought a dispatch to the General Station that Lee had surrendered his whole army to Grant and we sent in a flag of "Truce" to inform the Rebel Gen. of it. As we had them cut off from the main army of Lee's consequently they could have no communication with him, and did not know what he was doing. After a conference between our Generals they surrendered; if they had not we would have annihilated every one of them. This was the "Great Battle of the War," and will ever be remembered by all that was engaged in it. It is my last battle thus far, and I hope I can always say that it was my last battle. It was fought at the

Appomattox Court House. We encamped on the Battlefield for the night, only the field between us and the Rebels, some of our boys went across and talked to them.

Monday April 10th
Only yesterday war only was the main spring of action but today how different the times.

"Peace has been proclaimed throughout the state." It is only the "Echo of the hearts of the people, who were afraid to express their sentiments openly, if they did it would be at the risk of their lives." We withdrew our forces this morning, not having occasion to be there any longer, as the whole of Lee's army is held as prisoners of War, "Subdued at last Thank God," We took up our line of march towards Petersburg and the Appomattox Crt. Hse., a dilapidated looking place. I saw Lee's army encamped on the sides of a hill a short distance off. All gobbled by the "Dough faces and Yanks of the North," who a short time ago would hardly wipe their feet on.

Tuesday April 18th /65
Resumed our march early this morning and marched hard til we came in sight of Petersburg, and went into camp a mile outside of the city, at ½ past 2 o'clock, and close to the fortification which the Reb's had the city securely fortified against all attacks from us as they thought, but how nicely we showed them their mistake. They know not the real strength of our armies till within the past year. Then they found it out by experience, and a hard teacher it has been to some. We [illegible] their lookout which they had erected to watch our movements from the top of it. It is quite an extensive structure and very high. The country for 6 or 8 miles out of the city is splendid and very level but completely sacked, the houses all along our march today were not, the chimneys are the only vestiges of houses left to mark where they had once stood. The Negro huts were left standing…not being worth the time of firing them. The others had been burned some time ago. This evening I took a walk to and around the fortifications. There are two lines of them and before each is a trench 16ft wide and 8ft deep and partly filled with water. It would have been almost an impossibility for us to have taken the city at this point. We are in the rear of the city.

Wednesday April 19th
I have been busy making out affidavit of horses lost in battle and other ways. I used up all the paper and then stopped. I have just finished reading

the assassination of President Lincoln. It is a sad affair indeed to think that as soon as the fruits of his administration was beginning to show themselves, and while yet on the top most round of the ladder (that he had so steadily and surely mounted step by step), receiving His work that He should be cut down; or rather matched from the height he had gained to the skies to remain forever and ever, released from the cares and troubles of this world. It is all for the best, I judge. "What is to be will be." There is a guard placed outside of the city so that we cannot get in to see it. We have had a very pleasant day, are more comfortably fixed now than we have been since we broke camp on the 28th March. I read the account of the President's Death in the enquirer. He was shot through the back part of the head on the 14th of April and died on the morning of the 15th at 22 min past 7 o'clock. The funeral is to take place today between 11 and 3 o'clock. He is to be taken to his home in Springfield, Illinois. "A Nation mourns a National Loss, the Second Father of his Country."

Friday Ap. 21st /65.
I went into Petersburg again this morning. I had rather a harder time than I had yesterday to get in. They were getting more strict now, on every road there is mounted guards posted with drawn sabers and they stop everyone that comes up and those that have a h[orse?] can go on but the rest have to turn back. I had no h[orse?] but got in for all, there is more than one way of doing a thing. I rode down along the river to see the steamboats, sloops, and vessels, up this river they bring our rations and forage. It is very narrow but the tide was up here, so that steamboats and vessels are enabled to run up without much difficulty. You can buy most anything you want here by paying 3 or 4 prices for it. The fish market is very brisk, shad are plenty and selling at $.75 and $1.00 per price. Cheese; sugar .40 cts pound, coffee is a scarce article, onions; 10 piece, everything else in comp. When I got back to the Regt the boys were all saddled up ready to move, but we only went a ¼ of a mile then pitched our tent again. It is not quite as nice a place as we had before, but have to be satisfied with the chance. Look which way you will you see nothing but tents, the country for miles, around is while with them. And in the evening, the air is alive with the music from the different bands, nearly all of them playing at the same time and till pretty late in the evening. Our band is acknowledged by all to be one of the very best they have a very good selection of music. My favorite is a plain waltz they play. They have 15 pieces or instruments of music.

Mon. April 24th

We broke camp this morning at 42 past 7 o'clock and took the Petersburg and Boydton plank road to North Carolina where we are going to help Gen. Sherman, annihilate Gen. Johnston. Gen. Phil Sheridan is the boy that can do it too. He with staff and scouts passed us at noon. The scouts are few in number to what they were when I first saw them. I gave one of them my blouse to put on at the battle near Burksville Junction while we were drawn up in line to make a charge. He said that he wanted to have something blue on to go in the charge as he was dressed in a full Rebel suit. If one of them is caught, it is instant death to them. We tra[veled?] through Dinwiddie at 11 o'clock, it is 10 miles from Petersburg, through a splendid part of the country today and met a great many persons (principally negroes) with their all, enrout for Petersburg. Towards night we crossed the Nottaway River, it is nothing more than a good sized creek. Heavy cannonading was heard at intervals during the day and this eve, in a North Westerly direction, went into camp at 6 o'clock after marching 28 miles.

Thurs Ap 30th

I rode over to the 104th Reg't this morning to see a couple of my acquaintances Serg't Hampton and Will Johnson. We all went down in the city to see the sights. It has after a dilapidated appearance, the lower portion of it along the wharf (it is on the Appomattox River) is in ruins, most of the principal buildings and the Rail Road across the river are burned down, taking fire from our shot and shell, while others are pierced full of holes from them but not burned. The residents in that part of the city packed up and left in a hurry, some going out in the country, they being afraid to stay in the city at all. I was told that a great many persons even [illegible] from the bursting shells. Since our forces have occupied the place business has been quite brisk. The streets are alive with soldiers, both Rebel and our men, and also Negroes without number. There are not many citizens to be seen yet they are afraid to show themselves. There is a great many fine buildings in the town both private houses and places of business, but they all bear the marks of neglect and guilt a number are unoccupied. It is situated in a hollow and curtains 5 or 6 churches, also a very fine building used as a post office. I expected to be taken up every minute by the patrol, but luckily I escaped them. This afternoon I have been busy writing letters and making out monthly returns.

Sat. Aug 19th

At last we signed the rolls and marched right up to the [prepmaster] window to get our discharges and pay. At 11 I got mine and then struck a bee line for the Hotel at dinner and then got aboard of the 1.30 train for Phila. Pens. in an uncommon good humour with myself and things generally. I arrived here at 5.30 where just six months and four days ago, I left for the purpose of being one of the Actors in the great strife, which at least is ended. Thank God. This ends my service in the Volunteer Army of the United States. I can hardly realize yet that I am once more free to do, act, and go where I pleased, being so accustomed to being under the rules and regulations of those over you, that it is like a caged bird that is set free, and hardly knows which way to fly at first. I think rather more of myself since I came back to think that I did lend a helping hand and done my duty unflinchingly. And now if I am not too much demoralized, I hope to become a useful citizen and help build up our nearly ruined country so that Peace, Prosperity, and Harmony may exist throughout the land from Maine to the shelf of Mexico, and from the Atlantic to the Pacific. Fines,

[Signed] *J Lehman Eisenbrey*
Lumberville

18

From Private to Doctor

Following his life in the Civil War, Joseph Lehman Eisenbrey was more determined than ever to continue his education and start a family. At twenty-three, Eisenbrey studied dentistry, and for a number of years, he was a clinical instructor at the Philadelphia Dental College. Though it is unknown when Joseph decided to study dentistry in Philadelphia, he did, however, begin studying the practice just prior to his enlistment in the American Civil War. According to the *Dental Cosmos, A Monthly Record of Dental Science,* he practiced dentistry in the Philadelphia region for over thirty years and was known as one of the most "expert and successful men in his profession."

J.L. Eisenbrey was one of the original members of St. Martin's-in-the-Fields Protestant Episcopal Church of Chestnut Hill as well as a member of the Independent Order of Odd Fellows, the General George G. Meade Post and several dental organizations, including the Odontographic Society of Pennsylvania and the Pennsylvania State Dental Society. In 1879, Eisenbrey became president of the alumni association of the Philadelphia Dental College. Several of his dentist offices were located in Philadelphia, including a practice at Tenth and Race Streets, one at 141 North Tenth Street, and another at 1101 Arch Street. He also established a partnership with Professor J.E. Garretson at Fifteenth and Chestnut Streets. Married to Mary Bradley of Boston, who hailed from a prominent Philadelphia family, the couple was happily situated in their home located on the 8300 block of Seminole Avenue, Chestnut Hill, a few miles outside of Philadelphia.

The Eisenbreys had a son, Arthur Bradley Eisenbrey (who later became a surgeon), as well as a daughter (her name is unknown). However, as time went on, Joseph Lehman Eisenbrey suffered from "nervous prostration," according to his doctors. He traveled to Florida with hopes of relieving his condition. Unfortunately, following his return to Philadelphia, his health had severely declined, and on August 20, 1895, as his family sat down to breakfast, Eisenbrey shot himself with a rifle, with the bullet passing directly through his heart.

> *He possessed unusual ingenuity in meeting the difficulties presented by complicated cases in practice. His attitude toward his patients, and his gentle but firm sympathetic treatment of them, strongly attached him to his clientele.*
>
> —Dental Cosmos

PART V

The American Revolutionary War: The Continental Army in Bucks County and the Battle of Crooked Billet

Throughout the Revolutionary War, General George Washington and his army marched through various areas of Bucks County, but prior to reaching New Jersey for the monumental, and historic Battle of Trenton in 1776, he and his army would need to make their way across the icy, snowy Delaware River in harsh conditions. Though these men had just experienced an extremely tough loss in New York a couple of months before they reached Trenton, New Jersey, they persisted through the severe wintry conditions, ultimately winning the Battle of Trenton and continuing to fight for the cause of freedom.

On December 26, 1776, General George Washington and his tired, but still determined, army devised a plan to cross the Delaware River to attack the Hessian outposts stationed in Trenton. Despite the odds against them, Washington and his army defeated the Hessian forces, significantly improving his and his army's morale, inspiring reenlistments to join the cause and fight for freedom—and America.

In 1917, the Bucks County Historical Society, alongside the Daughters of the American Revolution (DAR), the Patriotic Order of the Sons of America and the Historical Society of Pennsylvania (HSP), urged the Commonwealth of Pennsylvania to establish the Washington Crossing Park Commission. Recognized less than a year later, the five-hundred-acre park is also home to restored colonial buildings such as the McConkey Ferry Inn, illustrating how our county's ancestors lived during the eighteenth and nineteenth centuries.

19

THE REVOLUTIONARY WAR

During the eighteenth century, York Road, or State Route 263, was the only road running between Philadelphia and New York, giving it its name. The easiest way for troops to travel through the area and cross the Delaware River en route to New York was through Bucks County. Along their way, many soldiers and generals, including Washington, made stops at several structures that are still standing today. The Continental Army passed through the county several times, as well as on their way to two important battles: the Battle of Trenton in 1776 and before the Battle of Monmouth, New Jersey, in June 1778.

The patriotism of the men from and around Bucks County continues to be written about in many history books. They led the revolt against the British Crown alongside the thousands of men from the Continental Army, and their courage is hard to surpass. With Bucks County being just a short drive from Philadelphia, birthplace of the nation, tourists flock to the area to experience what the Continental Army witnessed during its time in the historic county, from taverns and restaurants to inns and unmarked mass graveyards. Other sites of Revolutionary War battles and encampments are just a few miles outside of Bucks County, including Trenton, Princeton, Brandywine, Germantown, Monmouth and Valley Forge. On several occasions, the Continental Army, with Washington leading the way, marched through Bucks County, either greeting enemies on battlefields or seeking refuge in what are now inns and parks. Not only did the county provide the Continental Army with thousands of soldiers, but it was also home to three signers of the Declaration of Independence—Taylor, Morris and Clymer.

When the American Revolutionary War first began, a small number of Bucks's population remained loyal to the British Crown, some enlisting to fight alongside Major John Graves Simcoe, arguably the most harsh, brutal British commander of that time. Bucks County was one of the first counties to act when called for enlistment. However, many Quaker Friends were opposed to the war from the beginning because of the guarantee of bloodshed and tragedy. Many young Quaker men ultimately joined the cause, including several from Bucks: Janney, Linton, Brown, Shaw, Minor, Hutchinson, Bunting, Stackhouse, Canby and future general John Lacey.

When the Continental Congress authorized an army, Quaker John Lacey of Buckingham formed a company of sixty-four men in January 1776. The company's first lieutenant was Buckingham resident Samuel Smith. Among other locals who joined the cause are Robert Sample, a scholar from Buckingham who was later promoted to captain in Lieutenant Colonel Adam Hubley's Tenth Pennsylvania Regiment, and Alexander Graydon of Bristol, a captain in Colonel John Shee's Third Pennsylvania Battalion who later found himself imprisoned at Fort Washington, New York. Colonel Robert Magaw's roll of wounded, captured and deceased at the Battle of Fort Washington lists that Adjutant Johnson of Buckingham and Lieutenants Matthew Bennett and John Erwin were held as prisoners for several years. Other local men killed or captured at Fort Washington include Major John Beatty of Warminster, Lieutenant John Priestly of Bristol, Lieutenant William Crawford of Warrington, Timothy Knowles of Northampton and over forty more Bucks County men. Four Bucks County regiments were organized following the start of the war.

Isaac Van Horne, ensign, Solebury
John Wallace, sergeant, Warrington
John Murray, sergeant, Bristol
Robert Forsyth, corporal, Warrington
Richard Hay, private, New Britain
John Stevens, private, Bristol
John Banks, private, New Britain
Thomas Bell, private, Bristol
Daniel Gulliou, private, Warwick, died of wounds
Joshua Carrigan, private, Bristol, died in prison
Ralph Boon, private, Bristol

Ralph Aiken, private, Warminster
William Jenkins, private, Warwick
Robert Frame, private, Bristol, died in prison
William Huston, private, Warwick
Joseph Bratton, private, Bristol
James McNiel, sergeant, Bensalem
John Evans, sergeant, Bensalem
Daniel Kenedy, sergeant, Bristol
William Kent, private, Bensalem
Cornelius Foster, private, Bensalem
John Bell, private, Bensalem
Edward Murphy, private, Bensalem
Andrew Know, private, Bensalem
Halbert Douglass, private, Warrington
John Lalbey, private, Solebury
Edward Hovenden, ensign, Newtown
John Coxe, sergeant, Bensalem
Thomas Stevenson, sergeant, Newtown
John Sproal, corporal, Newtown
John Eastwick, corporal, Newtown
Richard Lott, private, Plumstead
Dennis Ford, private, Middletown
John Murphy, private, Falls
Thomas Varden, private, Glassworks
Richard Arkle, private, Wrightstown
Henry Aiken, private, Wrightstown
Charles A. Moss, private, Northampton
John Dunn, private, Falls
John Kerls, private, Falls
John Ketchum, private, Bensalem
Hugh Evans, private, Southampton, died in prison
George Clark, fifer, Biles Island (enlisted)
Reading Beatty, ensign, Warminster

According to William W.H. Davis, this is a list of the men from Bucks County in Colonel Magaw's regiment killed and captured at Fort Washington.

20

Washington Crosses the Delaware

*Christmas day at night, one hour before day is the time fixed upon for our attempt
on Trenton. For heaven's sake keep this to yourself, as the discovery of it may
prove fatal to us, our numbers, I am sorry to say, being less than I had any
conception of—but necessity, dire necessity will—nay must justify any attempt.
—General George Washington to Colonel Joseph Reed, December 23, 1776*

In 1776, Washington announced his plans to cross the Delaware and asked that the militia be ordered toward Trenton, New Jersey, and the boats collected west of the Delaware. At that time, Washington sent Colonel Humpton, commander of the Eleventh Pennsylvania Regiment, to collect the boats and General Putnam to construct rafts of lumber at Trenton. The Pennsylvania Militia was ordered to act as backup for Washington. On December 3, Washington and his army reached Trenton and crossed on Sunday, December 8, taking up temporary residency at Mrs. Berkey's house, approximately a mile from the river. A few hours later, the enemy, who had planned to cross the river, were shocked to discover that the boats had been moved to the west bank, prompting them to make demonstrations to cross at other points of the river including to Coryell's Ferry. General Greene was given command of Washington's army's safety. On December 10, General Greene was at Bogart's Tavern in Centreville, now Solebury, and he ordered General Ewing to send sixteen Durham boats to McConkey's Inn. Any boats that could not be secured had to be destroyed for fear that the British would

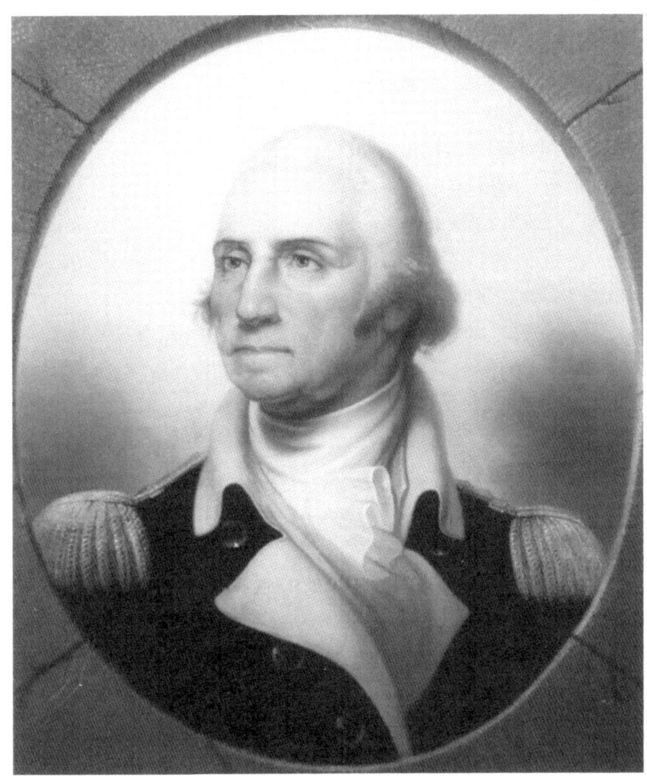

Portrait of General George Washington by American artist Rembrandt Peale. An adaptation, by the artist, completed circa 1858. *The Met Museum, Bequest of Charles Allen Munn, 1924.*

seize them. Boats were collected in Tinicum for the passage of General Lee's troops who would join Washington and his men shortly thereafter. In Attleborough, now Langhorne, on the last Thursday in December, the New Jersey legislature was summoned to meet at Four Lanes End to "take action on the future."

On December 9, General Washington sent four brigades under Lord Stirling, Mercer, Stephen and De Fermoy along the Delaware to station between Yardley and New Hope. Stirling took post at Beaumont's in Solebury with three regiments, and De Fermoy was at Coryell's. General Cadwalader was stationed at Bristol, and Colonel Nixon and his regiment were posted at Dunk's Ferry in Bensalem. Washington ordered the brigades to retreat to Germantown if driven from their positions. The supplies remained in Newtown, the county seat, as it sat far enough from the river and was easily accessed from all points.

It is said that, throughout his time in Bucks, General Washington had several headquarters in the county; however, he was not quartered at Newtown until after the Battle of Trenton. On December 15 and 16, there was a letter signed by Washington written from the Keith House, saying that his troops were "entirely naked, and so thinly clad as to be unfit for service."

Little evidence indicates when or where Washington conceived his plan of re-crossing the Delaware to attack the Hessians, but, the details were refined at the Keith House. All preparations prior to the crossing, including the selection of troops and boat collection, were kept secret. Troops from Pennsylvania, Virginia and New England were among those chosen to cross the river, and officers told to accompany Washington included Greene, Mercer, Stirling, Knox, Monroe, Hamilton, Stephen and Hand. Cadwalader was to remain stationed near Bristol to attack the enemy at Mount Holly, New Jersey. The troops were provided with cooked rations to last three days and forty rounds of ammunition. Thomas Paine's *American Crisis* was read to every regiment in General Washington's army to boost their spirits and confidence prior to the battle.

One day before the attack, the Hessians celebrated Christmas morning as Washington and his men made final preparations for battle. At Princeton, General Grant heard news of the forthcoming attack and advised Colonel Rahl of the Hessians, but they treated it with indifference. That same evening, a Tory from Bucks, said to have been one of the infamous Doan Outlaws,

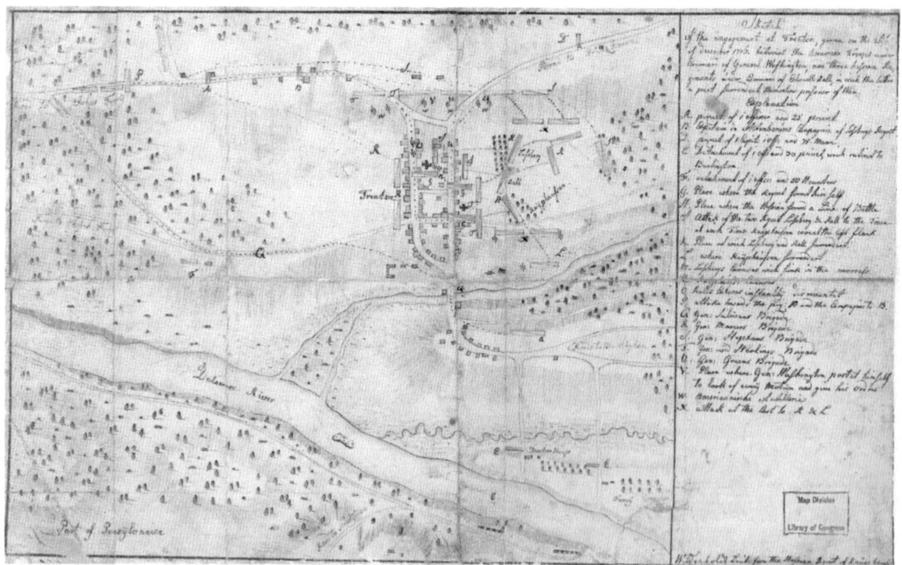

A Hessian sketch of the 1776 Battle of Trenton. Andreas Wiederholt. *Library of Congress, Rochambeau Map Collection.*

crossed the river with a note, advising them once more of Washington's plan. The note, which was placed in Rahl's pocket, was later found following the battle and his death.

According to W.W.H. Davis in *The History of Bucks County*, when Washington's men reached the outposts of Trenton on December 26, 1776, they had to ask a local about the Hessians' whereabouts. Unaware that General Washington was standing in front of him, the man responded, "I don't know." When one of Washington's men, Captain Forrest of the artillery, responded, "You may tell for that is General Washington," the man dropped his axe and exclaimed, "God bless and prosper your Excellency; the picket is in that house, and the sentry stands near that tree there," initiating the attack. Over one thousand prisoners and one thousand stands of arms and cannon re-crossed the river that afternoon heading toward Newtown, where the officers were quartered at the taverns and soldiers in the nearby church and jail.

In 1777, the Continental Army at Neshaminy consisted of nearly eleven thousand men comprising four divisions—Greene, Stirling, Stephen and Lincoln—dividing into eight brigades. Most of the men were encamped at Carr's Hill, Warminster, while others were stationed at Jamison and Ramsey Farms on Bristol Road. The Neshaminy Church was most likely used as a hospital, making it a prime location for a camping ground surrounded by a predominant Scots-Irish population. It was at this time that General Washington made his headquarters the Moland House on York Road in Warminster. The Moland House served as his headquarters while he awaited additional information about a large British fleet spotted off Delaware Bay. During this stay, the Marquis de Lafayette joined Washington's army as major general. On August 23, General Washington, Lafayette and the Continental Army marched through Philadelphia and continued on to the Battle of Brandywine.

On the Old York Road in Warwick Township…stands a substantial stone dwelling. In it Washington made his headquarters from the tenth to the twenty-third of August, 1777, and the local traditions and papers relating to the events of those thirteen days are not devoid of interest. The house stands beside the road about one hundred and twenty yards from the northeast end of the present bridge over the Little Neshaminy Creek, at the foot of a long and rather steep elevation known as Carr's Hill; and about half a mile above the village of Hartsville, formerly known as the Cross Roads. Within its walls many important dispatches were written,

*and Generals Greene, Lincoln, Stirling, and Lafayette, as well as Pulaski
and others, gathered under its roof.*

—William J. Buck,
Washington's Encampment on the Neshaminy

After six months of encampment at Valley Forge in 1777–78,
Washington and his men set forth toward New Hope through Doylestown
in their pursuit of New York. General Lee led the advance alongside his six
brigades. General Washington encamped at Doylestown on June 20—the
same night General Lee crossed through the town. The troops occupied
three encampments in Doylestown: one on the south side of State Street,
another on the ridge east of the Presbyterian church and a third along
the New Hope Pike east of the borough mill. General Washington set
up his tent near Jonathan Fell's farmhouse in Doylestown. According to
several records, the army was accompanied by the Oneidas, Tuscaroras
and warriors of the Seneca Nation who were seeking the release of their
captured chief. On the twenty-first, Washington's army resumed its journey
for the Delaware and crossed at New Hope the following day.

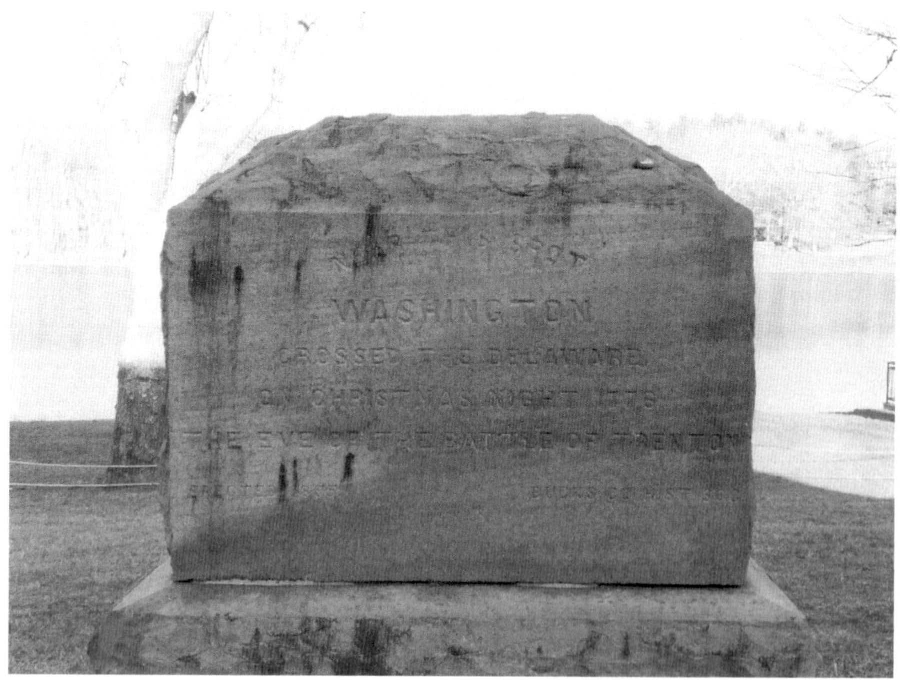

"Washington Crossed the Delaware on Christmas Night 1776, The Eve of the Battle of
Trenton." Historic marker, Washington Crossing State Park.

Despite the large number of men opposed to the British Crown, quite a few joined the opposing side. Edward Jones, of Hilltown, raised a company in Hilltown and New Britain; Evan Thomas of Hilltown commanded a company in the Queen's Rangers under Simcoe and participated in the Battle of Crooked Billet; Joseph Swift of Bensalem became an officer of the British army in the Pennsylvania Loyalists; Thomas Sandford commanded a company of the Bucks County Dragoons; and Walter Willett of Southampton served as a lieutenant of cavalry in the same company as Sandford.

21

General Washington's Headquarters

General Washington and his headquarters staff traveled together throughout the duration of the American Revolutionary War. His staff initially consisted of military secretary Colonel Joseph Reed and four aides-de-camp: William Palfrey, Stephen Moylan, Robert Harrison and Richard Cary. Headquarters staff managed official correspondence, made copies of the general orders that were distributed each day to the commanding officer at every military post and also made copies of individual orders made by General Washington. Together, he and his staff often stayed at military camps, taverns and houses belonging to rebel civilians or Continental Army officers. Usually, the headquarters operated out of a dwelling offering favorable geographical features. By utilizing general correspondence and expense reports, researchers have been able to determine where General Washington stayed during his time in Bucks County, such as the Moland House. As a note, some reports did not list a house, indicating that Washington set up camp on an owner's property or vacant land.

Summerseat, Morrisville

Summerseat, a beautiful homestead built in 1765 in Morrisville, Bucks County, was owned by both Robert Morris and George Clymer, two of the signers of the Declaration of Independence as well as the United

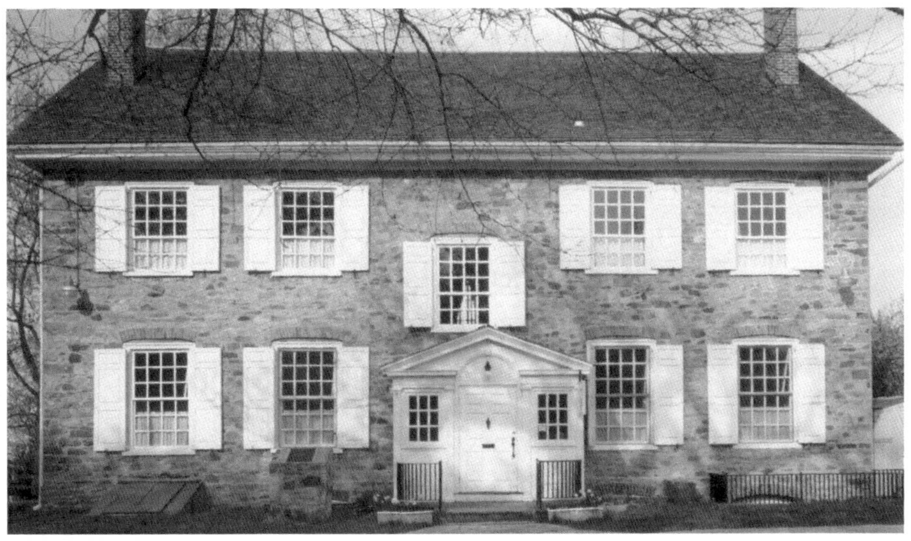

Summerseat, General George Washington's headquarters, December 8–14, 1776. Morrisville, Bucks County.

States Constitution. The house was constructed by Adam Hoops—one of the colony's wealthiest men. General George Washington made his headquarters at Summerseat and remained there from December 8 through 14, 1776. While at Summerseat, Washington issued a directive to his men prior to their famous crossing of the Delaware: "All boats and water crafts should be secured or destroyed." Charles Willson Peale, painter of George Washington, camped on the same property while Washington made the house his headquarters. Throughout 1776, several members of the Continental Congress decided to plot against the commander in chief because they believed he was a failure. Numerous Continental generals rode through Summerseat, including Thomas Mifflin, Lord Stirling, Henry Knox and Cadwalader, among others.

While Washington was residing at Summerseat, the property was owned by Thomas Barclay, who would later become America's first overseas consul and negotiate the nation's first treaty with a foreign country. Both Thomas Jefferson and John Adams recommended him for the honorable position. Records indicate that General George Washington sent twenty letters from Summerseat while encamped at the home.

Colonel Reed would inform you of the intelligence, which I first met with on the road from Trenton to Princeton yesterday. Before I got to the latter, I received a second express informing me, that, as the enemy were advancing by different routes, and attempting by one to get in the rear of our troops, which were there, and whose numbers were small, and the place by no means defensible, they had judged it prudent to retreat to Trenton. The retreat was accordingly made, and since to this side of the river…in the disordered and moving state of the army, I cannot get returns; but, from the best accounts, we had between three thousand and three thousand five hundred men, before the Philadelphia militia and German battalion arrived; they amount to about two thousand.

—*Washington to the president of Congress, Sunday, December 8, Summerseat*

John Harris House

John Harris's house in Newtown, Bucks County served as General Washington's headquarters immediately following the Battle of Trenton during the Continental Army's winter campaign. Reportedly arriving the morning of December 27, 1776, Washington took up quarters in Harris's house while his troops were likely sent back to their former camps prior to the battle. Washington remained at the house for at least two days prior to gathering the same troops he had initially crossed the Delaware with and crossing once more. As a thank-you, General Washington gave Harris's wife a silver teapot that had remained in his family's possession for several years. The teapot was later turned into spoons.

Lord Stirling, major general of the Continental Army, remained in Newtown. Records indicate that Stirling was too "unfit" from the Battle of Trenton to continue offering his services to the army.

John Moland House

John Moland, born in London in the early 1700s, was commissioned as king's attorney in Pennsylvania. A landowner in Warwick Township in 1737, Moland also purchased just over three hundred acres in Rockhill Township, Upper Bucks County, from Thomas Freame, the husband of Margaret Penn, daughter of William. He then married Catherine

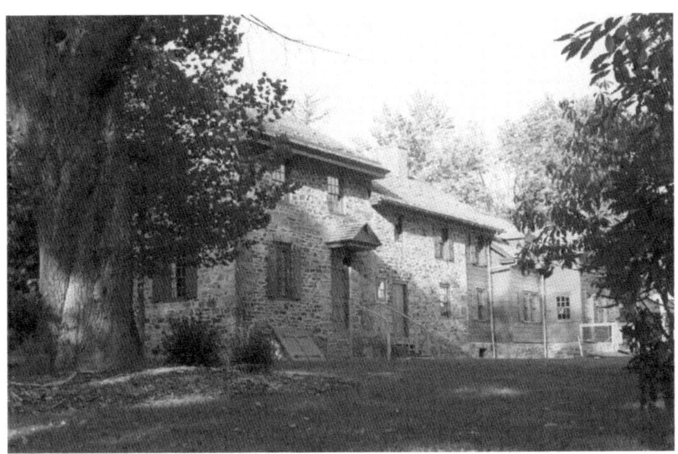

The Moland House. Warwick, Bucks County. Original portion was built by John Moland in mid-1700s. The Moland House served as General Washington's headquarters in August 1777.

Hutchinson of New Castle, Delaware. In 1740, John Moland petitioned for admittance as an attorney for the court of common pleas in Newtown. Over the course of the following two decades, Moland appeared in several records at the county courthouse, often being referred to as a justice. Two years later, he became known as being one of the Philadelphia Bar's most qualified members. Dying just a few years before the start of the Revolutionary War, John left his wife with their children. Two of their sons would become directly involved with the war—one would join the Continental Army, while the other would choose to fight for the British Crown.

William Moland, who chose to fight for Washington, became well educated in the medical field, serving as a surgeon during the war. Some say William worked alongside Washington during numerous battles, including some of the most influential in the area. In early 1778, William visited his brother in the West Indies, seeking financial help. Upon his return, he was charged with high treason by the Pennsylvania Supreme Executive Council for entering through British-controlled Philadelphia prior to visiting his brother, despite his involvement in the sixth class of the Continental militia in Plumstead Township. William, knowing that his father had studied law with John Dickinson, requested a pardon. On September 5, 1788, Moland was granted a pardon, but the council labeled him as an "imprudent young man who cared little about the cause of the Revolutionary War." In 1785, he owned over one hundred acres in Warminster Township before becoming an alcoholic, according to testimony made by his wife, and spending the remainder of his life at the almshouse in Warwick Township.

From August 10 through 23, 1777, the Moland House served as headquarters for General George Washington on his way to the famous Battle of Brandywine. It was here that Major General Marquis de Lafayette requested to join the Continental Army. Despite General Washington's initial refusal, Lafayette soon became a member of the army, fighting fearlessly alongside his American comrades. Washington's encampment reached from Old York Road to both sides of Bristol Road from Mearns to Meeting House Roads. The Battle of Crooked Billet also took place near the property on May 1, 1778.

THE KEITH HOUSE

The Keith House is a historic homestead located in Upper Makefield, Bucks County. The house served as General George Washington's headquarters for ten days, from December 14 through December 24, 1776. The homestead, which was erected in the mid-1700s, encompasses over two hundred acres of land originally owned by William Penn for his family but was later sold to a group of investors in 1697. The land was acquired by William Keith in 1761 through auction. The Keith House was listed in the National Register of Historic Places in 1978 for its pivotal role as Washington's headquarters just days before the Battle of Trenton in 1776. The Keith House was owned by the Keith family for over 130 years. In 1893, following the death of John Keith, the house was sold to John Paxon.

It was at the Keith House where General Washington planned his monumental crossing of the Delaware River and his attack on the Hessian forces at the Battle of Trenton. According to legend, the homestead's springhouse held John Honeyman, a spy for the Continental Army. Honeyman, despite having served the British during the French and Indian War, became sympathetic to the American cause and approached George Washington, offering his services as a spy. General Washington is said to have contacted Honeyman for a meeting at Fort Lee, New Jersey, to discuss his plan to attack the Hessians at what would later become the Battle of Trenton. Honeyman was accepted by the enemy garrison in Trenton, acting as a Tory, for his previous service he provided the British.

According to prominent historian William W.H. Davis, the Keith House is a two-story stone house, consisting of a pine door set in a solid oak frame. Davis also suggested that, at the time of his writing, the same wooden lock was still being used since Washington occupied the home. It was assumed that Washington used the front room on the first floor for an office, sleeping in the room above it. In a letter to Brigadier Generals Lord Stirling, Mercer, Stephen and De Fermoy, General George Washington wrote the following instructions prior to the Battle of Trenton from the Keith House on December 14, 1776:

Lest the enemy should in some degree avail themselves of the knowledge (for I do not doubt but they are well informed of every thing we do), I did not care to be so particular in the general orders of this day, as I mean to be in this letter to you. As much time, then, would be lost, should the enemy attempt crossing the river at any pass within your guard, in first sending you notice, and in the troops to wait for orders what to do, I would advise you to examine the whole river from the upper to the lower guard of your district; and, after forming an opinion of the most probable crossing-places, have those well watched, and direct the regiments or companies most convenient to repair, as they can be formed, immediately to the point of attack, and give the enemy all the opposition they possibly can. Every thing in a manner depends upon the defense at the water's edge. In like manner, one brigade is to support another, without loss of time, or waiting for orders from me. I would also have you fix upon some central spot convenient to your brigade, but in the rear a little, and on some road leading into the back road to Philadelphia, for your unnecessary baggage, wagons, and stores; that, in case your opposition should prove ineffectual, these things may not fall [into the enemy's hands] *but be got off, and proceed over Neshaminy Bridge towards Germantown, agreeably to the determination of the board of officers the other day.*

Let me entreat you to find out some person, who can be engaged to cross the river as a spy, that we may, if possible, obtain some knowledge of the enemy's situation, movements, and intention. Particular inquiry to be made by the person sent, if any preparations are making to cross the river; whether any boats are building, and where; whether any are coming over land from Brunswic; whether any great collection of horses is made, and for what purpose. Expense must not be spared in procuring such intelligence, and it will readily be paid by me. We are in a neighborhood of very disaffected people. Equal care therefore should be taken, that one of these persons does not undertake the business in order to betray us. I am, dear Sir, yours, George Washington.

—Online Library of Liberty, a Collection of Scholarly Works about Individual Liberty and Free Markets

22

THE BATTLE OF CROOKED BILLET

General John Lacey of Buckingham became a military officer during the American Revolution when he was appointed brigadier general in the Pennsylvania Militia in January 1778. Lacey, member of a local militia unit that was incorporated into the Pennsylvania Line of the Continental Army, fought in several major battles, including Matson's Ford and Germantown, as well as the skirmish at the Crooked Billet.

In December 1777, General Washington and his men had moved to Valley Forge for their winter encampment. Just a few months later, General Lacey took command of his militia and would exchange many letters with Washington over the course of 1778. There is much debate over the strength of Lacey in the Continental Army—some attest that he was not fit to be a general.

After Lacey's appointment to the position, Washington sent him two objectives to meet by spring 1778: guard the roads leading to Philadelphia and protect the Patriots throughout the countryside. General Washington feared that the British would raid Bucks County and the surrounding areas, capturing or killing leaders and locals. The British offered a large sum for farming tools and produce that would supply their troops with food during their winter encampments, so Washington removed the ability to travel into the city without good reason. Lacey suspected several locals to be Tories who would make it into Philadelphia, often joined by the Pennsylvania Loyalists or Bucks County Volunteers. In a letter to Washington, Lacey wrote:

I have now under Confinement Twelve persons all taken going into Philad'a at different times with small parcels of Marketing on their Backs. I have just reason to suspect the greatest part of them, as they are young fellows, are going to join the Enemy in Capt. Thomas Company of Refugees, as they call themselves. I am informed that parties are now out in Bucks County collecting as many of that stamp as they can find, which in my opinion will be no inconsiderable number.

—George Washington from Brigadier General John Lacey, February 27, 1778

Lacey's fears were not unjustified. In February of that same year, over thirty Philadelphia Light Dragoons under Captain Hovenden joined forces with forty men from the Bucks County Volunteers and raided a fabric mill, capturing thirty-four Continental guards and killing several men. The British stole enough fabric to clothe five hundred soldiers.

General Lacey's camp continued to shrink despite the Supreme Executive Council's promise of one thousand men at all times. Over the course of a few months, Lacey's camp shrunk to six hundred men. However, General Washington received several letters from Lacey, writing to him about not-so-great news coming from his camp, including an accident in which six to seven thousand cartridges were damaged or destroyed from an explosion within a tent. The fire left five men with serious burns and the camp without blankets and thousands of cartridges. At one point, Lacey had but fifty men and horses. Overall, Lacey and his men were unprepared and weak compared to the Queen's Rangers in May 1778.

In Philadelphia, John Simcoe was ordered by British commander William Howe to facilitate the inhabitants bringing their produce into the city from Bucks County and surrounding areas. British and Loyalist troops led continual raids into Bucks County, despite Lacey's militia. In April, Simcoe gained permission to launch a surprise attack on Lacey in order to bring supplies into the city. Spies in Bucks County informed Simcoe that Lacey's army of fewer than five hundred men was camped at Crooked Billet. On April 30, the British sent out a joint force of Hessians and British troops in an effort to capture, or worse, slaughter Lacey's men. Marching from Philadelphia, the British continued to Second Street Pike through Huntingdon, up through Horsham, and turned down a road running from "the Willow Grove to the county line." At the first crossroads, the troops turned left and came to the county line near the red octagonal schoolhouse, located at the corner of York and Monument Avenues. The schoolhouse was established in 1834 by Henry

Eisenbrey (father of Civil War private Joseph, see chapter 4) and his brother, Peter. Marching through several fields, Simcoe and Abercrombie split up, with Abercrombie moving up Easton Road to join forces with Simcoe at Lacey's encampment. As Lacey retreated, Simcoe and several men passed across the farm of Thomas Craven and through the village of Johnsville onto Bristol Road, where they successfully escaped the pursuit. General Lacey's militia was completely taken off guard by the Queen's Rangers' attack, led by Simcoe.

While Lacey was still asleep, the British attacked the American camp in the early morning hours of May 1, 1778. General Lacey had ordered Lieutenant Neilson and Ensign Laughlin to patrol the area and report to him any news of the approaching British. Neither Neilson nor Laughlin left camp when instructed, allowing for the Queen's Rangers to take Lacey's men by surprise. Bands of British and Loyalist troops raided their camp, fighting near the Crooked Billet Tavern (its stone walls still exist at 57 York Road, Hatboro). With his camp virtually surrounded by the Queen's Rangers and entirely outnumbered, Lacey was able to pull his troops to a nearby wooded area. After repulsing a cavalry charge, his men had to withdraw further. The skirmishing continued for two miles until General Lacey's militia was forced into retreat into Warwick, losing all of their supplies, equipment and a number of men. Upon their return to camp, his troops discovered burned, dismembered bodies; many had been covered with straw and set on fire. It is unfortunate, yet worth noting, that the victims were most likely burned alive judging by their postures at death. According to W.W.H. Davis, on Thomas Craven's farm, in a field near the county line was a large heap of burnt bodies and buckwheat straw. Some speculate that the mass grave is located near what is now County Line and Madison Avenue. In an article printed by the *Royal Pennsylvania Gazette* (Philadelphia) on May 5, 1778, General Lacey's army lost eighty to one hundred men, between fifty and sixty men were made prisoners and ten wagons were stolen. The British did not lose one man but left with seven wounded.

Some of the unfortunate, who fell into the merciless hands of the British, were more cruelly and inhumanely butchered. Some were set on fire with buckwheat straw, and others had their clothes burned on their backs. Some of the surviving sufferers say they saw the enemy set fire to the wounded while yet alive, who struggled to put it out but were too weak and expired under the torture....Others I saw, who, after being wounded with a ball, had received near a dozen wounds with cutlasses and bayonets.

—a letter from General Lacey to Major General Armstrong

Lacey lost about 20 percent of his force either killed or taken prisoner as a result of the battle, as well as several wagons of necessary supplies. In his report to the president of the Supreme Executive Council of Pennsylvania, Thomas Wharton, Lacey reported that his troops were entirely surprised by the attack, as his scouts had "neglected the proceeding night to patrol the roads as they were ordered, but lay in camp till near day, though their orders were to leave it by 2:00 in the morning." The lieutenant leading the patrol, Neilson, failed to alarm the others of the danger, claiming that he was so near the British that if he fired, he would surely be "cut to pieces." According to Lacey, Neilson failed to patrol the area and instead left for his post at daybreak rather than two o'clock. Neilson was court-martialed and cashiered from the militia for disobeying orders. The dead were buried in at least one known mass grave near County Line Road, a short distance from "Craven's Corner." The wounded were cared for at the house of Thomas Craven and remained there until they recovered.

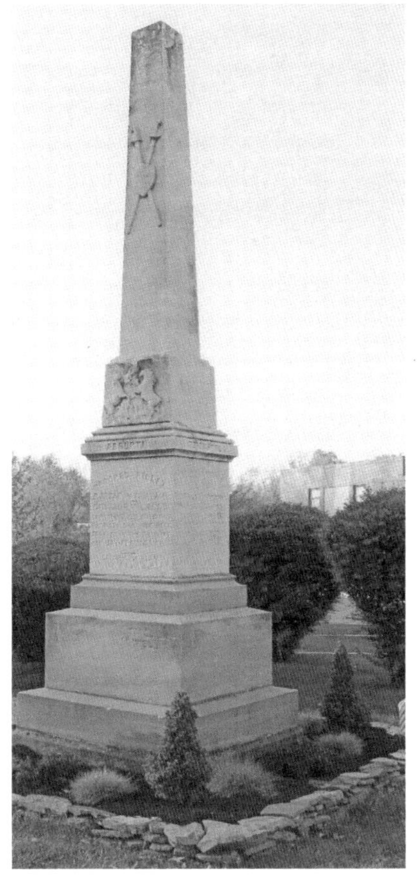

Battle of Crooked Billet monument, dedicated to those who fought the battle against the British. Hatboro, Montgomery County, Pennsylvania.

Reports soon surfaced that the British troops had committed atrocities during and after the battle. Six days later, General Washington ordered Brigadier General Maxwell to conduct an inquiry into the allegations so that a proper report could be filed with British commander General Howe. Bucks County justice of the peace Andrew Long took the depositions of four residents who witnessed the battle, including thirteen-year-old Safety Magee, Thomas Craven, Samuel Erwin and Samuel Henry:

In 1778 I was living with my uncle, Thomas Folwell, Southampton, in the house where Cornell Hobensack lives, on the road from Davisville to

Southampton church. On the morning of the battle I heard the firing very distinctly and a black man named Harry and myself concluded we would go and see what was going on. We started from the house and went directly toward where the firing was. When we came near where Johnsville now stands, we heard a heavy volley which brought us to a halt. The firing was in the woods. The British were in pursuit of our militia and chased them along the road that leads from Johnsville to the Bristol road, and also through the fields from the Street road to the Bristol road. They overtook the militia in the woods at the corner of the Street road and the one that leads across to the Bristol road. When the firing had ceased, we continued on to the woods, where we found three wounded militiamen near the road. They appeared to have been wounded by the sword, and were much cut and hacked. When we got to them they were groaning greatly. They died in a little while and I understood were buried on the spot. They appeared to be Germans. We then passed on and in a field nearby we saw two horses lying dead. They were British. One of them was shot in the head and the gun had been put so near the hair was scorched. While we were on the field, Harry picked up a cartouch box that had been dropped or torn off the wearer. Shortly after we met the militia returning and when they saw the black fellow with the cartouch box they became very indignant; charged him with robbing the dead, and took it away from him. These dead horses were on the farm of Colonel Joseph Hart. Soon after this we returned home. The last man was killed on the British road at the end of the road that comes across from Johnsville. A British officer, who was badly wounded at the battle of the Billet, was taken to the house of Samuel Irvin, who lived nearby. His wounds were dressed there and he afterward returned with the troop to Philadelphia.

—Safety Magee, Northampton Township

Inns and Taverns: Serving Up Ales and History

Spirituous liquors were sold along the Delaware as soon as the white man showed his face upon its banks, for strong drink invariably waits upon him in the wilderness. The earliest record on the subject goes back to 1671, when Captain John Carre, the English governor of the west bank of the river, licensed persons both to sell and distill spirituous liquors.
—William W.H. Davis

During the American Revolution, many Bucks County taverns and restaurants saw action from inside their own stone walls. Imprisoned soldiers would be held overnight, notorious generals and commanders would stop in for a pint, and some were meeting places for the Continental Army. General Washington and his men reportedly dined numerous times at McConkey's Ferry Inn (located in what is now Washington Crossing State Park) prior to the successful Battle of Trenton. Following the war, some officers found tavern license approval fairly simple. These establishments transitioned throughout the years, some providing shelter and food for the average traveler while also serving as gathering spots for community meetings.

For the traveler or local, a tavern was a place to rest, eat, drink and enjoy oneself for a moment or two of pure relaxation. In the early 1700s, when the first inns began to appear in Bucks County, particularly along the roads to New York, locals and travelers alike would flock to these businesses either alone or in groups. Bucks County, being the travel destination that it is and was, attracted thousands to the area for its rolling countryside and proximity to Philadelphia. Historic taverns and inns were usually accompanied by picturesque signs either displayed by a post in the front or by a swinging fixed sign attached to the side of the site. These signs were found all throughout Bucks County but have since diminished as society moved away from horseback.

The earliest known map of Bucks County by Thomas Holme in 1687 depicted roads laid out across the lower end of the county—including Bristol Road, which followed along a Native American path prior to 1677—and two additional roads on the west side, County Line and Street Roads, which run through the center of the area. A series of major highways were then planned to connect Philadelphia with the country farms and towns, including the Old York Road, which followed a Lenni-Lenape trail from Jenkintown, Willow Grove and Hatboro, Montgomery County, to Hartsville and Buckingham, Bucks County, in 1711, and Easton Road, which connected Horsham to Doylestown, Pipersville, Durham and Easton in the 1720s. Durham Road, which opened in 1683, ran north–south through Bucks County from Newtown to Bristol and was then extended through Wrightstown, Pineville, Buckingham and Ottsville until it reached the Durham Iron Furnace in 1746. These major roadways would open up the desire for inns and taverns across Bucks, with many of the original innkeepers and landlords being women or Quakers of good standing. In the early days in Philadelphia, a tavern license was restricted to widows and "decrepit men of good character" who had to circulate a petition to the court and governor for approval. In 1744, thirty people were licensed to operate a tavern in the county: Benjamin Harris, Joseph White and Malachi White of Bristol Borough; Eleazar Jones of Bristol Township; John Orr of Bedminster; Ann Amos and John Vandegrift of Bensalem; Benjamin Bering, New Britain; Eleazar Stackhouse and Mary Taylor, Middletown; John Rich of Plumstead; Joseph Thornton and Joseph Inslee, Newtown; Benjamin Canby, Solebury; Thomas Hamilton, Peter Snyder and Jacob Boyer of Rockhill; Peter Walbec and Jacob Moyer of Upper Milford; Richard Brink and Richard Thomas, Warrington; John Ogilby of Southampton; John Baldwin, Warminster; John Williams of Falls; Andrew Van Buskirk, Nicholas Pennington and Hugh Young of Wrightstown; and John Wilson of Tinicum, among a few others. In William W.H. Davis's 1876 *History of Bucks County*, he wrote that the tavern locations of several of the aforementioned owners were well known at the time. Joseph Thornton of Newtown operated the still-standing Brick Hotel, and Hartsville native John Baldwin owned a tavern prior to him leaving Warminster, located at York and Street Roads in Warminster, also presently in operation. In 1748, Bernard VanHorne Jr. of Northampton, according to documentation, had "no regard to the laws, encouraged drunkenness," allowed fighting and gaming on Sundays and reportedly "beat his wife in an extraordinary manner." Six years later, thirty-five other Bucks County residents petitioned for licenses, including John Strickland and Lawrence Hoff of Southampton. In 1761, Thomas Cooper also petitioned, remarking that the locals of a neighborhood at Bristol and York Roads in Warwick required a public house. His proposal was rejected in 1765 as there was evidence of a tavern in the same area in which he petitioned. Daniel Craig opened a tavern at Newville, then Warrington but present-day New Britain Township, called Craig's Tavern. Remaining in operation through the late nineteenth century but under management of Jacob Markley, the tavern became a well-established hostelry and was often celebrated for its offerings of bountiful meals and choice top-shelf liquor.

By 1830, there were over 128 licensed inns or taverns in Bucks County alone. In the nineteenth century, Pennsylvania was credited with having more inns and taverns than any other colony or state in the country, which makes perfect sense as the northern traders and southern plantation owners would have to cross the Pennsylvania border to reach the other territory.

The King's Road, or what is now Bristol Pike, connected Philadelphia with Morrisville just opposite of Trenton, New Jersey. One of the earliest mentions of this road was at a court held in Philadelphia in 1683: "King's Road from the Schuylkill River to the Neshaminy Creek be marked out and made passable for horses and carts when needed." Development and maintenance of the roadway was an arduous task that resulted in movement of the roadbed numerous times. Also known as the Bristol Turnpike, this roadway was considered the fastest and most direct route to New York. Along the way, taverns and inns were frequent stops for the thousands of travelers who passed through the region.

Second Street Pike, originally constructed as an extension of Second Street in Philadelphia, becomes Huntingdon Pike in Montgomery County, as well as Windybush Road where it meets River Road in New Hope. In Bucks County, the road runs through Southampton, Richboro and Wrightstown. Designed as a shortcut between Philadelphia and the ferry to New York at New Hope during the time of the stagecoach, Second Street Pike once had tavern signs swinging alongside the road reflecting typical American themes, rather than that of English heraldry, such as a buck, bear and eagle—all of which were easily found in Bucks County during the eighteenth century. Bears regularly fed Native Americans, deer were seen in herds galloping across the countryside and the eagle was a favorite political and well-known symbol of America.

Bucks County has had three county seats: Bristol (1705–26), Newtown (1726–1813) and finally Doylestown (1813–present). Lawyers and justices who frequented the county seat desired better food and service than a standard tavern or inn could offer. Taverns would concentrate on food and wine with rooms reserved for monthly rentals, and above the taproom sat a large room that often served as the community social hall. The taverns with regular customers would become more prosperous than those that relied on the local farmer or passing stagecoach. Nonetheless, competition still existed, leaving some to rise or fall based on the voting principles of a landlord, some never obtaining a liquor license because of local politics.

The Delaware River was the main point of travel prior to any of the roads that would help Bucks County flourish. The construction of the Delaware Division Canal began in 1827, but it wasn't until 1831 that the first barge could make the sixty-plus-mile run from Easton to Bristol. Prior to the Civil War, three thousand boats traveled along the canal, making New Hope the halfway point, the location of the toll collector. By 1931, the canal was abandoned by its operators to later become a public park, but not before it helped boost the local economy with the construction of numerous inns and taverns.

Easton Road, or the route to Easton, was important to Native Americans prior to the arrival of the English. The clans of the Lenni-Lenapes would meet the Shawnees from the Poconos and the Algonquins from New York in Easton. It was the Treaty of Easton in 1758 that forced the Lenapes to give up all rights to eastern Pennsylvania, pushing them west. Beginning in Willow Grove and heading through Doylestown and Pipersville, joining with Durham Road, Easton Road welcomed the electric trolley as a popular means of transportation from a few years following the Civil War until World War I. Trolleys connected many towns across the county, allowing for visitors and guests to stop for a pint at a local pub or tavern. These well-established taverns made Bucks County a popular travel destination as the years went on.

Old York Road, which splits from Easton Road in Willow Grove, Montgomery County, extends more easterly toward Hatboro, crossing Buckingham and ending just four miles shy of New Hope. In the late eighteenth century, the stage line began frequent service to Princeton, New Brunswick and other surrounding towns in New Jersey, connecting the Pennsylvania side of the Old York Road with its counterpart across the Delaware. This route was particularly important to traveling ministers and connected numerous Quaker meetings. During the nineteenth century, sections of the Old York Road were made designated turnpikes, allowing travelers to stop along their journey to savor a bite to eat.

Durham Road, which extends through the center of Bucks County, not only served the farmers in the midlands but also played a key role in carrying iron to the city from the deposit of ore and limestone in Durham. The ore and limestone supplied the Continental Army with the materials necessary to make rifles during the Revolutionary War. The same iron can be found in the ornamental cast details in Philadelphia houses of the same period. Durham Road originally stretched from Bristol to Newtown in 1693. Ten years later, the road was extended to Buckingham and again to Plumstead in 1726. By 1745, Durham Road ran past the Durham Iron Furnace. It is estimated that this route experienced more traffic than any other route to New York, allowing for many Bucks County taverns and inns to open shop along the way, most notably some of the oldest in the county: the Logan Inn, the Anchor Tavern, the General Greene Inn and Piper Tavern.

23

THE RED LION INN

The Red Lion Inn, also called the Red Lion Hotel, built in or around the 1730s, was a historic inn located near the Red Lion Bridge in Andalusia, Bensalem Township. The first public house in the area, the Red Lion Inn welcomed British and American armies for a pint and a meal throughout the Revolutionary period. Established by local Philip Amos, the inn remained in operation by his family for over forty years, petitioning the court to open a public house of entertainment "on the highway from Philadelphia to Bristol." In 1774, the Red Lion welcomed several delegates to the First Continental Congress who stopped by for a meal on their journey to Philadelphia, including Samuel Adams, John Adams, Bowdoin Cushing and Robert Treat Paine. John Adams, who became the second president of the United States, was also known to snag a bite on his frequent travels to Philadelphia. In 1781, General George Washington and his army camped behind the Red Lion Inn for a night on their way to Yorktown.

The center room on the upper floor was not heated but was often warmer than any surrounding rooms during the cold winter months. Throughout its lifetime, the historic inn saw some renovations, but many areas of the dwelling were left unchanged, including the grand fireplace in the basement around which many meetings were held during the American Revolution. In the nineteenth century, the inn was also known as a stop along the Underground Railroad.

The Red Lion Inn was located on the Kings Highway, or what is now Bristol Pike, at the bridge across the Poquessing Creek. The inn survived well over two centuries until it was destroyed by fire in December 1991. A few blocks away is the Hart Burial Ground, which was established in 1683. Many notable figures are buried at the cemetery, including several of Bucks County's earliest settlers and ancestors of Dr. Benjamin Rush.

24

THE FERRY INN

The Ferry Inn, also known as the Delaware House and the King George II Inn, located at the east corner of Mill and Radcliffe Streets in Bristol, is a four-story stone and frame inn first constructed in 1681 by Samuel Clift. Following his arrival from England, Clift received a grant of over 260 acres of land from Governor Andros of New York in March 1681. The grant was to become effective with William Penn's charter from England's King Charles II.

Charles Besonett, a local Frenchman, purchased the inn from Clift in 1735 during George II's reign. The structure that is still visible today replaced the original ferry house. Rumor has it that when General George Washington and the Continental Army approached the area, Besonett had the image of King George II painted over to resemble the commander in chief. The King George II served as headquarters for General Cadwalader in December 1776 when he and his troops were stationed at Bristol to help guard Washington during his winter campaign—some soldiers reportedly spent a lively evening at the bar. Records indicate that George Washington, John Tyler, John Adams, James Madison and Millard Fillmore were among the dignitaries who vacationed here. In the nineteenth century, Joseph Bonaparte, then King of Spain and brother to Napoleon Bonaparte, was a frequent visitor to the inn. Shortly thereafter, Bonaparte made his home in nearby Bordentown, New Jersey. Following the end of the American Revolution, the inn was renamed the Fountain House and became a popular destination as a summer resort; it was renamed the Ye Olde Delaware House in 1892.

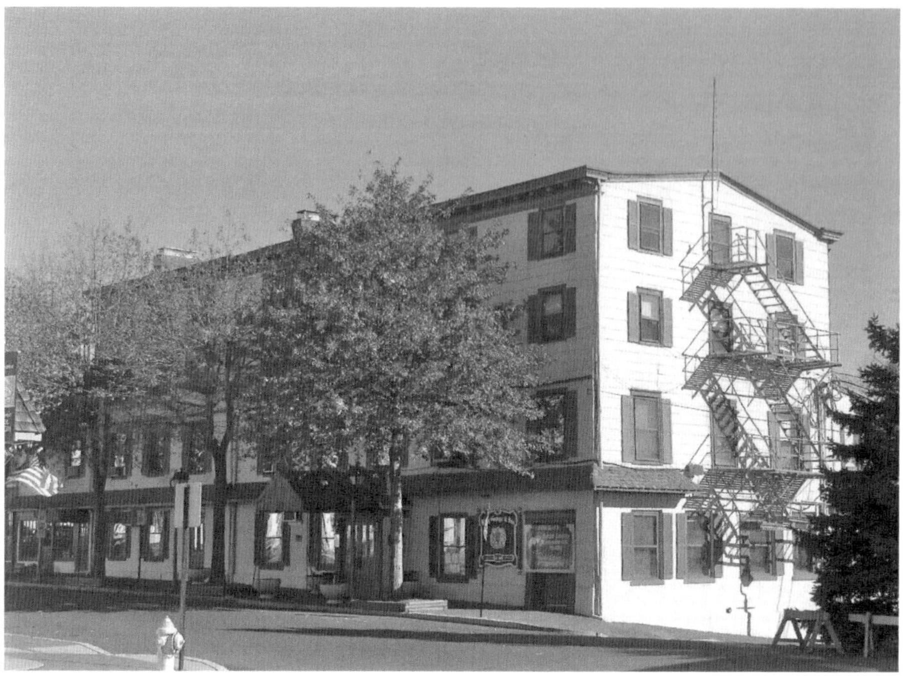

The King George II Inn, originally known as the Ferry House. Established 1681. Bristol, Bucks County.

Despite the renovations and additions the building underwent, the inn still maintains a historical feel, holding onto its integrity and significance. After the Revolution, the King George Inn gained a respectable reputation among both Continental and British officers for being one of the best inns between New York City and Philadelphia.

The bar sign is dedicated to the "merry souls who make drinking a pleasure, who achieve contentment long before capacity." Made from imported wood from the ship *Lafayette*, the original bar still stands, waiting for its visitors to enjoy a drink with a splash of history.

25

Dilworth's Tavern

lthough the date the inn was first licensed in Bucks County is unknown, records indicate that as early as 1758, the inn was called Dilworth's Tavern. Since its establishment in the mid-1700s, the tavern was the only watering hole in Warminster throughout the eighteenth and nineteenth centuries. The tavern and surrounding land was owned by Thomas Beans, owner of nearly two hundred acres in the area who inherited the property from his father, Isaac. He became proprietor and owner of the fastest horses in the country. Horse races attended by thousands of spectators occurred frequently on Street Road, with almost a half mile of track on his property. The tavern, which is now present-day Mike's York Street Bar and Grill, became a popular resort for sportsmen, with races being held several times a year. Despite several accidents, including the death of at least one horseman, the tavern remained in operation for several years. After twenty of his horses died of disease, Thomas was forced to sell his property at sheriff's sale. Isaac Beans, Thomas's son, resided in Hatboro, Montgomery County, and upon his death in 1814, he granted his residential property to his son John and the plantation in Warminster to his daughter, Margaret. Isaac had two other sons, Isaac III and Thomas, both of whom were also given property.

During the War of 1812, Bean's Tavern was a meeting place for locals who were drafted in the war. In William W.H. Davis's report on the county's involvement in the conflict, he wrote, "The quota from this county, consisting of 88 artillery and 814 infantry and riflemen, to be taken from the first and second classes of the enrolled militia, was called for the 12th of August. They were taken from the four old militia regiments, and consolidated into a battalion…assembled at Thomas Bean's Tavern, Warminster to march to Marcus Hook."

The tavern was a horse racing center for over a century. Horse races and militia trainings alike frequently occurred on the property and racetrack. It was a locally famous house of entertainment and hospitality under numerous landlords.

26

General Greene Inn

In 1752, Henry Jamison (b. 1729), his father and uncle from County Tyrone, Ireland, were granted a license for a public house by the Bucks County court. Under Jamison, the inn was in operation for nearly ten years. John Bogart, who later married Jamison's widow, became the owner of the inn from 1773 through 1777. Subsequent owners include the VanHorn and Wilkinson families.

In 1775, Bogart's Tavern became a regular meeting place for Patriots for nearly two years following a meeting organized by the Bucks County Committee of Safety to discuss its opposition to British rule. A receipt for £75 was sent by John Adams, assisting the group's first act: to support the committee of the town of Boston.

In August 1775, training for the Revolution was in progress at Bogart's Tavern. Robert Poque (or Polk) and John Shannon, two Patriots from nearby Warwick Township, visited the home of William Ely to borrow a gun to use in the muster. Shannon, who was giving the training exercise, accidentally discharged the gun, striking Poque in the throat, instantly killing him. The Poque, or Polk, family were large landowners near Hartsville and had immigrated to America from Carrickfergus, Ireland, in 1725. Some say that Robert was of the same lineage as President James K. Polk.

General Nathaniel Greene, a commander in Washington's forces at the Battle of Trenton, set up headquarters at Bogart's Tavern. On December 10, 1776, Greene ordered "sixteen Durham Boats and flats (constructed at nearby Durham Furnace) down to McConkey's Ferry" while staying at the

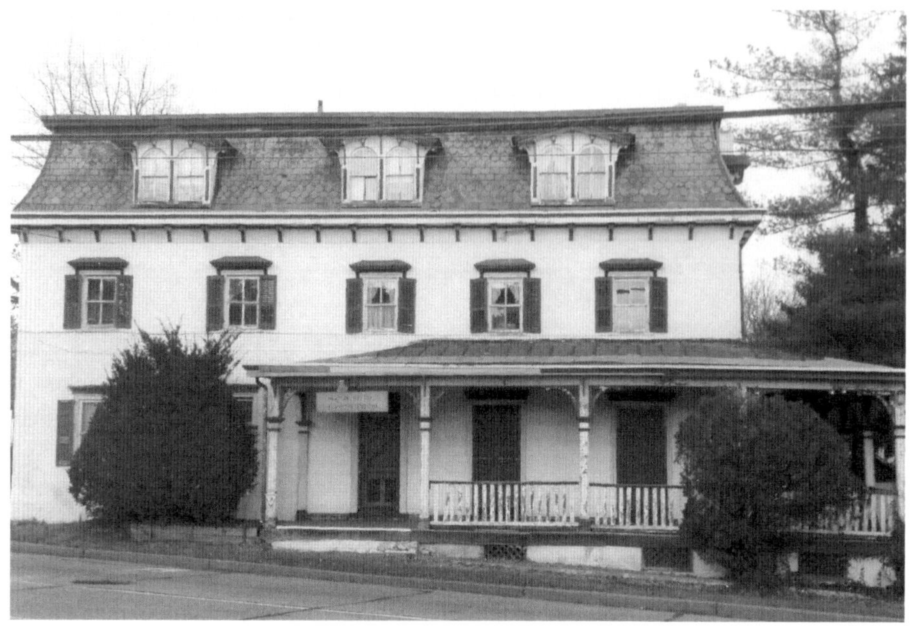

General Greene Inn, also known as Bogart's Tavern. Buckingham, Bucks County. The inn and tavern first opened for business in 1763 by Henry Jamison.

inn. These were the same boats Washington and his men used when crossing the Delaware in December 1776.

Throughout the years, Bogart's Tavern was also given several other names, including the Sign of George Washington, and the Sign of Penn's Treaty. Despite the tavern being remodeled during the late nineteenth century, the original walls still remain, as well as the "old grill room" that was used as General Greene's headquarters. The tavern remains standing, but is currently inaccessible to the public.

27

PIPER TAVERN

In operation from 1778 through 1823 by Colonel George Piper, founder of Pipersville, Bucks County, Piper Tavern sits near the intersection of Durham and Dark Hollow Roads. George, born near the Wissahickon River in Philadelphia on November 11, 1755, moved to Bedminster Township as a young adult and later to Pipersville after he wed Eva Lear, daughter of Arnold Lear, private secretary to General George Washington. In 1775, George opened a store in the town and later moved into the structure himself in 1778. Colonel Piper was an officer in the Continental Army and colonel in the Pennsylvania Militia. Piper also assisted General Paul Mallet Provost in purchasing a plot of land on the east side of the Delaware River that became the popular town of Frenchtown, New Jersey.

The tavern, constructed in 1759 by Joseph Bladen, was purchased by Colonel Piper in 1778. The tavern has fifteen-inch-thick walls, a parlor, a dining room, a large kitchen and several guest rooms for local travelers. Additions were made to the tavern in 1784, 1790 and again in 1801. Among those who stayed or were served meals at the tavern include Benjamin Franklin; General Lafayette, who stopped en route to a hospital to recover from wounds received in the Battle of Brandywine; Robert Morris and George Taylor, both signers of the Declaration of Independence; and Joseph Bonaparte, king of Spain, who brought along his own cook and table silver while vacationing at the tavern for nearly two weeks.

According to legend, Colonel Piper's wife, Eva, was quite the revolutionary herself. During the war, Eva dug up her inheritance, or about £325 in gold from the inn's cellar to support her husband's command by purchasing shoes and clothing for his men. The infamous Doan Gang entered the tavern while she was ironing and demanded money. Since George was away, Eva took it upon herself to break the arm of one of the brothers using the iron and chased the other away with her husband's sword.

Piper Tavern had many names, including Keichline's Tavern, the Upper Bucks County Hotel and Brugger's Pipersville Inn, when James A. Michener, Pearl S. Buck, Dorothy Parker and others visited. To this day, the restaurant owners pay tribute to the history of the tavern and Colonel Piper with the name Historic Piper Tavern.

28

THE SPINNERSTOWN HOTEL

Quakertown, Bucks County, is home to many historical landmarks, including the Spinnerstown Hotel, an inn that has been serving the public for over two hundred years. The Spinner family, for which the small village of Spinnerstown earned its name, received a 153-acre tract of land owned by a gentleman with the last name of Morris. In 1811, David Spinner Jr. obtained a license to operate a tavern near his family's property and ran the tavern for eight years until he was appointed justice of the peace in Quakertown. His father, David Spinner Sr., who was a famous craftsman and artist of German-inspired artwork, held the position prior to his son's appointment. David Spinner Jr. remained the owner of the property for over fifty years, renting it to several innkeepers in his lifetime. In 1857, Edwin Spinner, his son, named the tavern the Spinnerstown Hotel.

Serving as a resting place between New York and Philadelphia for many local travelers, the Spinnerstown Hotel preserved much of its charm and history and remains a staple in the community. The Dale family purchased the hotel in June 1959 and have since operated the hotel longer than any proprietors in its history.

29

McConkey Ferry Inn and Washington Crossing Inn

The McConkey family of Taylorsville, Bucks County, or what is now Washington's Crossing, were influential in helping the Continental Army's winter campaign and the Battle of Trenton in 1776. According to Washington Crossing Historic Park, the McConkeys ran the Old Ferry Inn, also known as the McConkey Ferry Inn, originally owned by the Baker family who had built the first structure on the same site and sold to Samuel McConkey, the same year as the monumental battle.

The first building was erected in 1752, but only the basement kitchen remains. Built in several stages, the current ferry inn represents what a standard tavern looked like throughout the years surrounding the American Revolution. In the late 1750s, the McConkeys operated both the Ferry Inn and the ferry crossing, welcoming General Washington as a guest before he headed to Trenton. During Washington's stay in Taylorsville, the inn was closely guarded by troops. Records indicate that the Hessian officers who were captured at the battle were imprisoned near the Ferry Inn.

Dear Sir: Notwithstanding the discouraging accounts I have received from Col. Reed of what might be expected from the operations below, I am determined, as the night is favorable to cross the River, and make the attack upon Trenton in the morning. If you can do nothing real, at least create as great a diversion as possible. I am sir,
Yr. most obt. Servt.,
George Washington, McConkey's Ferry, 25th December, 1776,
—letter addressed to Colonel Cadwalader

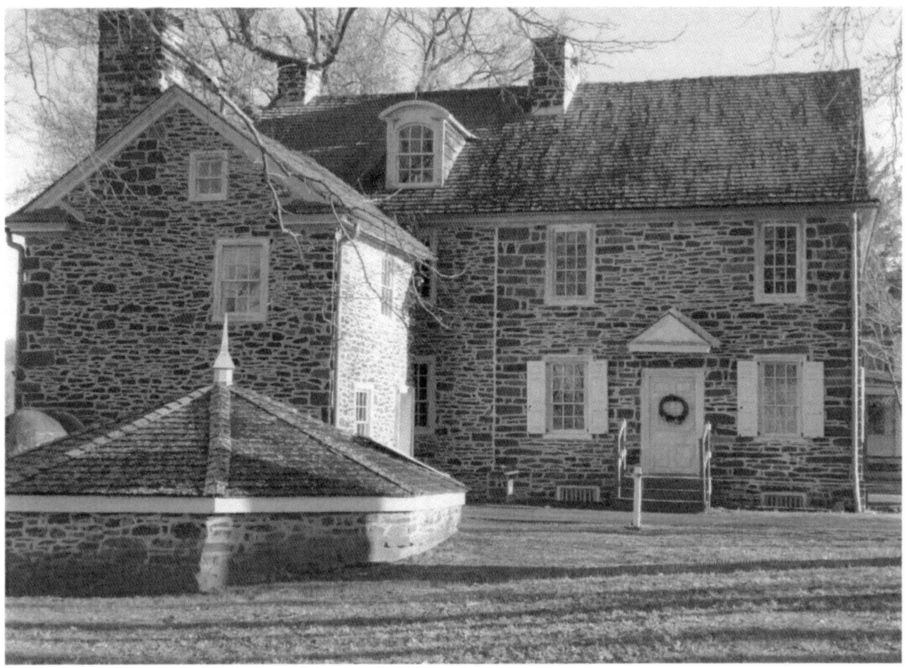

McConkey Ferry Inn. Washington Crossing Historic Park. The Ferry Inn is one of thirteen historic buildings that comprise the lower park.

In 1777, the Ferry Inn was sold to Benjamin Taylor III, including over three hundred acres, all of which are included in what is known today as Washington Crossing. Mahlon, Benjamin's son, operated the Ferry Inn, while his other son, Bernard, ran the ferry service and formed a fishery. A section of Washington Crossing Inn, now a popular stop for a night out on the town, was built as the Taylors' homestead in 1817. The stone building contains a kitchen, dining room and two bedrooms on the second floor. The kitchen's open hearth remains today and is the reason behind the name of the Hearth Room of the restaurant. Other areas of the house were constructed in the 1840s. The homestead remained the family's possession for one hundred years.

In 1919, the Commonwealth of Pennsylvania designated the area along the Delaware to commemorate Washington's famous crossing in 1776, changing the name of the town from Taylorsville to Washington Crossing. About ten years later, the Haven family, owners of the Old Ferry Inn, purchased the Taylor homestead, renovating it and adding the colonial-style addition that is now the ballroom and lobby. The Hearth Room and

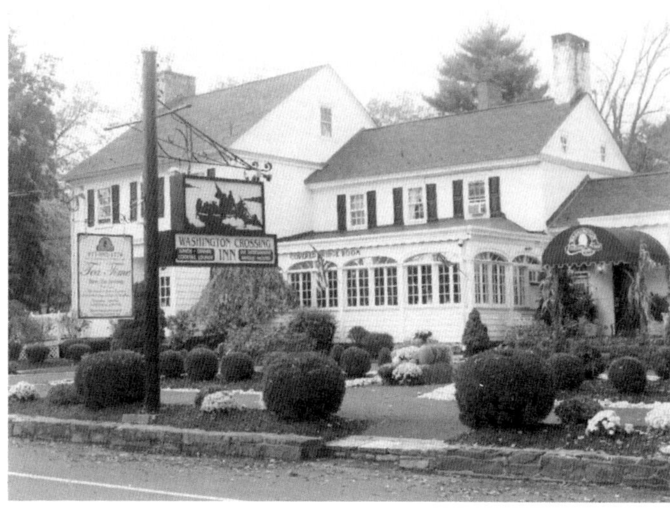

Washington Crossing Inn. Washington Crossing, Bucks County. Sections of the home were built in 1817 by Bernard Taylor.

Covered Bridge Room were both sections of the original home restored as the restaurant's dining areas. Dr. Eli Mordechai and Jerry Moradi currently own the Washington Crossing Inn, preserving yet another remarkable piece of Bucks County's history.

30

Black Bass Hotel

uilt around 1745, the Black Bass Hotel, originally known as the Lumberville Hotel by locals, welcomed thousands of guests, including many celebrities and prominent figures. The inn, which served as a retreat for travelers and traders alike, is located in Lumberville, Bucks County, formerly known as Temple Bar. The old tavern contains a large open hearth, a taproom and décor that transports guests into the eighteenth century.

In the nineteenth century, mules were readily on hand to facilitate movement for canal operators. In 1831, a fire erupted, burning sections of the tavern to the ground. The landlord, Major Anthony Fry, opened the cellar doors and removed a stash of gunpowder being stored there. Had Major Fry not responded so quickly, the Black Bass Hotel would have met a much different fate.

According to the Black Bass's current owners, General George Washington did not stay at the inn while preparing for his famous crossing of the Delaware. The innkeeper was in fact a Tory, and Washington was reportedly turned away from a night's stay while in town. However, there are several tales surrounding the property, some involving spirits that never checked out of the inn.

Two tales specifically revolve around the canal. In the early nineteenth century, many immigrants, particularly those of Ireland, arrived in the area to build and work on the Delaware Canal. Hans, owner of the Black Bass at the time, was fatally stabbed by one of the workers visiting the hotel. There

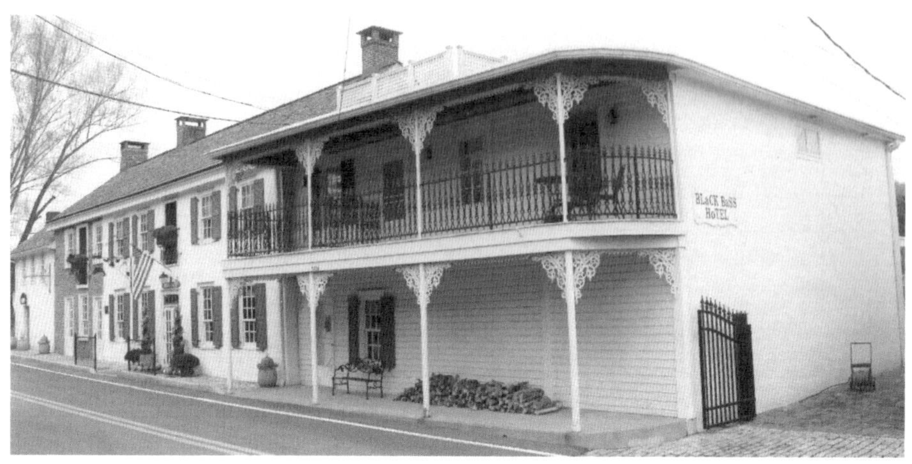

The Black Bass Hotel, Lumberville, Bucks County. Circa 1745.

have been several reports of guests seeing Hans standing in the corner of the tavern. The barstool he was sitting on when he was murdered is reportedly still at the tavern.

Irish workers who dominated the canal work this side of the Delaware, as well as in New Jersey, died during the cholera epidemic of 1832—some also passed of severe exhaustion. Many of these workers were subsequently buried in unmarked graves along the canal. Research has shown that a few of the deceased were placed in a makeshift morgue near the tavern and were stored there until a boat arrived to retrieve the bodies. Some have reported unexplained drops in temperature, while others have told stories of hearing heavy crying or weeping from the morgue area.

Another tale involved a woman that guests have witnessed wandering halls and sitting, holding a pearl-handled revolver in a guest room, perhaps the one she stayed in. Rumor has it that the woman found her husband sharing a room with his mistress, and out of distress and heartbreak, she shot and killed both of them before turning the gun on herself. Along with the sightings, guests have also smelled the faint scent of lavender accompanying her spirit.

President Grover Cleveland, Liza Minelli, Ethel Merman, Marlon Brando, Carlos Santana and Christian Slater, as well as several English lords and ladies, are among those who stayed at the hotel over the years. In 2008, the inn was purchased by Jack Thompson, local patron of the Black Bass and owner of several automotive dealerships in the county, who restored and retained the hotel's history as much as possible.

31

TEMPERANCE HOUSE

In 1772, local soldier and schoolmaster Andrew McMinn, who was "fond of whiskey," built the first section of a house as a tavern and a schoolhouse. The land on which it sits was originally deeded to Shadrach Walley, Newtown's founder, by William Penn. It operated for nearly forty years until 1813, when the Bucks County seat moved from Newtown to Doylestown.

In 1746, a temperance movement made its way through Newtown, beginning with a petition signed by 31 citizens. The petition's goal was "to suppress certain public houses which are public nuisances and very prejudicial to some neighbors…and are not supplied with suitable conveniences to entertain travelers." While owned and operated by McMinn, the inn served as a gathering spot for Continental soldiers fighting in the Revolutionary War. In 1835, the tavern was reopened by borough constable, auctioneer and member of the Newtown Temperance Society Chillion W. Higgs, who named it the Sign of the Good Samaritan. It was during this time that few alcoholic beverages were served, just mineral water, lemonade and the occasional glass of mead. In 1848, under new proprietor William Hallowell, the tavern was renamed the Temperance Hotel. In 1865, when the property was owned by Joseph Willard, Edward Hicks, a Newtown resident, artist and Quaker preacher, inspired the tavern's next name, the Niagara Temperance House, creating a sign that was painted with a moose next to the Niagara Falls. In 1871, the business changed hands (and names) again when Willard's brother, Sam, purchased

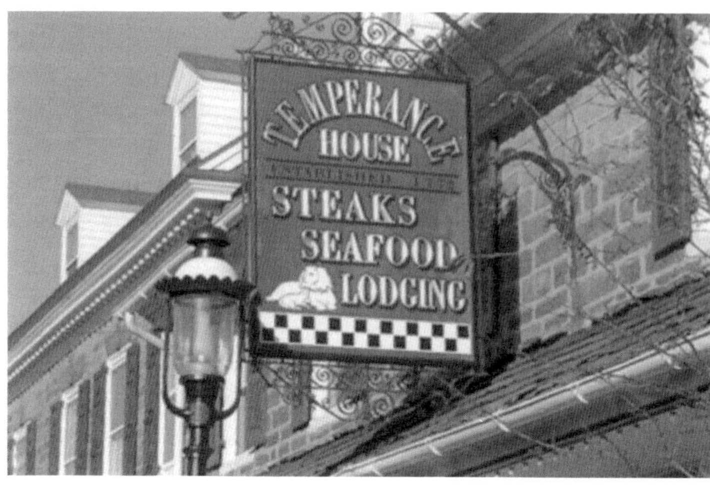

Temperance House tavern sign. Newtown, Bucks County.

the tavern and renamed it the Temperance Hotel Oyster and Ice Cream Bar (the Temperance House, for short).

An advertisement for the hotel and tavern was listed in a local paper: "The proprietor of the Temperance Hotel…hereby informs his friends and the public generally, that he is now prepared to furnish them with ice cream either in large or small quantities."

In 1965, the tavern began offering alcohol again under new owner H. Clifford Neff. The Temperance House is still open and operating as a tavern and inn, the present owner making special effort to retain the historical significance of the property.

32

McCOOLE'S AT THE RED LION INN

At the intersection of Broad and Main Streets in Quakertown sits McCoole's Red Lion Inn. Originally opened in 1750 by Walter McCoole, it was known as McCoole's Tavern during the Revolutionary War and later as the Red Lion Hotel in 1793. The tavern, the first built in Quakertown, was used as a meeting place in 1799 during the Fries Rebellion and became a popular place for locals and organizers to discuss the rebellion against a tax to fund a war with France. During this period, the first Germans were arriving to the area with hopes of finding plenty of harvest and farming opportunities, as well as religious independence. The Germans believed the tax was part of a plan to assist in the establishment of a British monarchy in the United States. John Fries organized a rebellion after several protesters were arrested; the prisoners were freed, and all organizers and protesters returned home.

Alexander Hamilton declared that the protesters were guilty of treason and were to be hanged opposite of the Red Lion Inn. President John Adams learned of the arrest and pardoned the protesters.

As Quakertown grew larger, the inn followed directly, expanding in 1810 and then again in 1865, creating several rooms for guests wishing to spend a night or two at the inn.

33

THE LOGAN INN

The Logan Inn, located in New Hope, Solebury Township, was established by the town's founder, John Wells, in the 1720s, and it is arguably one of the oldest continually operating inns in the country. John Wells ran a ferry from Pennsylvania to New Jersey, providing the inn its original name, the Ferry Tavern. New Hope was once named Coryell's Ferry after a ferryboat that operated between there and Lambertville, New Jersey, by ferry operator John Coryell. The ferry played a role during the Revolutionary War in June 1778 when the Continental Army crossed the Delaware prior to the Battle of Monmouth. In 1790, tragedy struck when a disastrous fire destroyed the mills in the town. Once the mills were rebuilt, the town was renamed New Hope.

The Ferry Tavern offered aid to General George Washington and his army during the war, providing him and his men a place to sleep, eat, drink and tend to their injured. Unfortunately, the Continental Army was reportedly forced to store the deceased in the basement due to the wintery conditions outdoors. In the 1820s, a bridge was built connecting Pennsylvania with New Jersey, and the ferry ceased service. On February 22, 1828, a town-wide celebration occurred in honor of Washington's birthday, and on this day, the inn was named the Logan Inn. The name change was in honor of a Lenni-Lenape chieftain called Wingohocking, who is depicted on the sign swinging outside of the property. Wingohocking grew incredibly fond of James Logan, William Penn's secretary, and therefore adopted his name. The original sign was reportedly purchased by the townspeople, who collected funds to pay for it out of appreciation

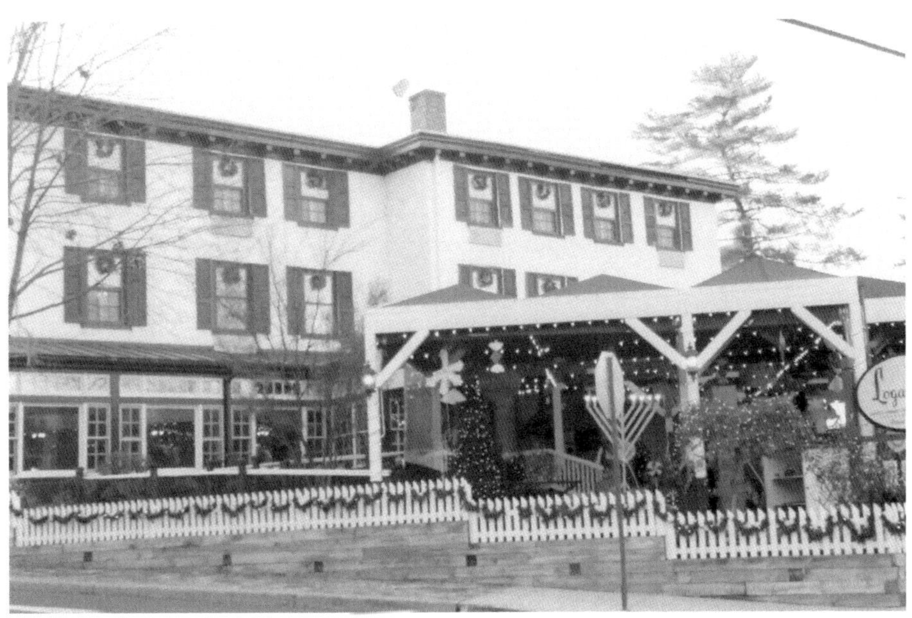

The Logan Inn. New Hope, Bucks County. Established in about 1727. One of the oldest continually operating inns in America.

for the chieftain. Over the course of its lifetime, the inn was also known as Coryell's, Canby's and Beaumont.

A few haunted tales have also survived alongside the inn, several involving soldiers of the Revolutionary War. During the war, many of the deceased soldiers from nearby camps and battles were brought to the Ferry Tavern's basement for storage, as previously mentioned. There have been several reports that a man dressed in a Revolutionary War uniform, assumingly of the Continental Army, appears for just a short moment or two in front of guests and inn staff, leaving a "cold air pocket" before disappearing in the oldest areas of the inn: the basement, dining room and bar. It is thought that the man was presumed dead and was carried to the basement for storage. He later awoke in excruciating pain from his injuries, unable to cry or shout for help, dying from his wounds. Another entity is often seen on the second floor wearing what appears to be another uniform from the Revolution. However, he is never seen with a head—only his body, torso down, has appeared for visiting guests. Among several other tales, the spirit of a Hessian soldier, who was perhaps killed in the Battle of Trenton, haunts the basement of the inn. One particular theory explores the idea that the Continental Army refused to allow his body to be eaten by animals, bringing in his body along with their own.

PART VII

The Horrific Train Wreck that Rocked Bucks County to Its Core

Search was continued for several additional bodies thought to be in the debris of the wreck near Bryn Athyn…yesterday which so far has claimed a toll of 25 lives and injured seriously more than a score.
—Wilkes-Barre Times, *December 6, 1921*

On December 5, 1921, a deadly train wreck occurred in a rock-sided curve between the Upper Southampton, Bucks County and Bryn Athyn, Montgomery County train stations, carrying many local residents. Trains numbered 156, 151 and 154, also a milk train, the two passenger trains operated by the Philadelphia and Reading Railway, collided head-on while traveling at full speed in the Bryn Athyn section in Upper Moreland Township. However, the crash itself did not cause the most deaths—the flames, which shot through and engulfed the train cars, trapping several dozen people inside, caused significant suffering with many lives lost.

The railroad between Newtown and the city of Philadelphia was a determining factor in the development of what is now Upper Southampton Township, previously a crossroads, dry good store, post office and several residences. However, after the inauguration of the railway, the village became a bustling town that began commuting nearby residents to Philadelphia, and vice versa for those who sought a stay away from city life. Built in 1892, the Southampton Train Station consisted of a ticket office and a waiting room on the first floor and living quarters for the stationmaster on the second. The Newtown Line remained the only steam-operated commuter line in the Philadelphia region.

34

THE WRECK

On a cold, wintry morning, the local #151 northbound passenger train traveling from Philadelphia to Newtown was given an order from the local stationmaster at nearby Huntingdon Valley to pull off to the side at Bryn Athyn near Fetter's Mill Road because two trains, the morning milk and express train #154, and passenger train #156 from Newtown, both having just passed the Southampton Train Station, were heading south on the same track, toward #151. Tragedy became inevitable when the train's engineer and conductor misunderstood the orders and continued north after #154 passed, not realizing the #156 was still on the track, rapidly approaching. Due to the snowy conditions at the time of the wreck, neither the engineer nor the conductor were able to see the red signal down the track. During this same time, Russell Clayton, the stationmaster at Bryn Athyn, received a call from the Huntingdon Valley office to ensure #151 pulled off for the express—he was unaware that there was an express heading toward #151 and immediately phoned Woodmont Station at Byberry Road to order them to hold #156. Unable to stop either train from their unavoidable fate, Clayton notified local authorities of the imminent tragic event.

According to reports made by surviving passengers, both trains were near or exceeding the speed limit of twenty-five to thirty miles per hour when they met in the curve, neither train having visibility of the oncoming until it was far too late to slow down or stop. The impact caused #151 to flip #156's engine upside-down, the coals in the gas tanks catching fire to the wooden coaches. The engine of #151 ran atop of #156 and crashed into Pennypack Creek. The coaches from both trains were soon engulfed, leaving many unable to evacuate in time. The crash occurred in a narrow passage between two steep rock walls on each side of the track, making it more difficult for the passengers to escape. Rescue workers struggled to reach those who were trapped due to the terrain, flames and weather conditions. Surrounded by intense fire and nearly ten inches of snow on the ground, twenty-seven died and seventy were injured—many of those who died were burned to death.

> *The first crash did not kill many but the death total rose as the flames reached the helpless victims imprisoned in the wreckage.*
> —*the Associated Press, December 5, 1921*

The crew of #151, specifically the conductor and engineer, were held responsible for the wreck and forced to remove themselves from their jobs. According to the *Wilkes-Barre Times Leader* published the day after, three investigations were helmed by the coroner, State Public Service Commission and railway officials. "The railroad company issued a statement saying that the crew of train No. 151, northbound, over-ran orders." The tragedy made headlines around the country, including the cover of the *New York Times*. It was this tragic accident that prompted wood-framed passenger cars, subsequently nicknamed "coffin cars" by the public, to be banned across America. Despite being one of the most dreadful train wrecks to occur on the East Coast, the event is not widely known. Many of the bodies, some unidentifiable, were reportedly

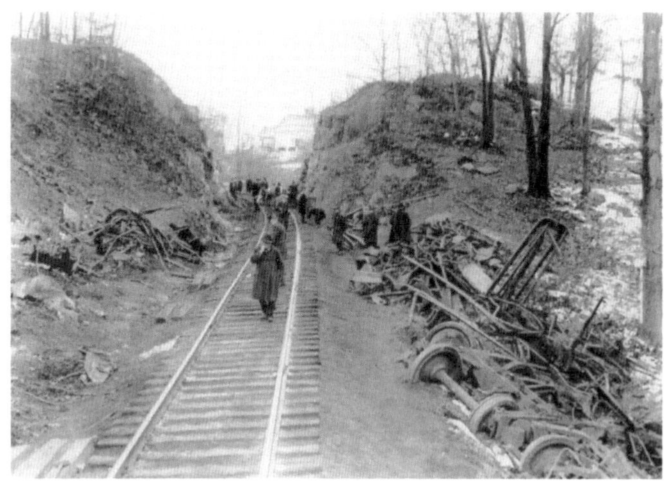

Actual photograph from site of the train accident that killed twenty-seven people; many were residents of Bucks County. *Historic Langhorne Association.*

buried in a mass grave at a nearby cemetery in the Churchville section of Southampton off of Bristol Road. The train tracks carried passengers until the mid-1980s until SEPTA, or Southeastern Pennsylvania Transportation Authority, shut down service on the Newtown Line, one of the last rail lines built in the nineteenth century. The Southampton Train Station, which is still standing today, was subsequently closed.

On February 18, 1922, Charles Evans, conductor, and Walter Yeakel, engineer, were this afternoon found guilty of negligence in connection with the Bryn Athyn wreck on the Philadelphia and Reading Railway last December in which 26 persons were killed. The jury recommended mercy. Pending motions for a new trial the two men were released. The jury was out more than twenty hours, and took about two hundred ballots before a verdict was reached.

—Harrisburg Telegraph, *February 18, 1922*

35

THE AFTERMATH

An article in the *Wilkes-Barre Times Leader* dated December 6, 1921, graphically described the tragedy and provided the names and details of those injured and deceased:

Railroad Crash Thus Far Claims Toll of 25 Lives—More than Score Hurt

Search was continued for several additional bodies thought to be in the debris of the wreck near Bryn Athyn…yesterday which so far has claimed a toll of 25 lives and injured seriously more than a score.

The wreck occurred on the one track Newtown Division of the Philadelphia and Reading Railway when two passenger trains, Nos. 151 and 156 collided head on, on a sharp curve walled in by high ledges of rock…

…Identification of some of the bodies was almost impossible because they were burned to crisps when the old-fashioned wooden coaches burst into flames immediately after the crash.

Many of the bodies were so badly mangled that they had to be picked up in pieces in baskets. Many Roasted Alive…. Very few passengers if any escaped death in the first coaches of both trains. The riders in these coached if not killed outright were roasted alive as the flames overtook them.

No. 151 left Reading Terminal here at 6:48 a.m. and No. 156, leaving between Newtown for Philadelphia at 7:30, being late, the first train was to have waited on the siding at Bryn Athyn for the southbound train to pass.

Orders to this effect were said to have been handed to Conductor Evans at Bryn Athyn. Railroad officials said it was the duty of the conductor to communicate these orders to the engineer which was said not to have been done...

...When No. 151 pulled out of Bryn Athyn without waiting for 156 to pass the station agent, knowing what the orders were, and being too late to stop the train, immediately put in a call for ambulances at nearby hospitals being certain of what was to happen.

List of Identified Dead.

John Crusen, 6, Newtown; Elmer Hanson, Newtown; Dr. Irvin J. Hatch, Newtown; Miss Elizabeth Shelmire, Southampton; Louis Johnson, Southampton; Mrs. Katherine Fitzpatrick, Southampton; Thomas Gove, Philadelphia, fireman on No. 151; Edward Vogel, Ryers, fireman on No. 156; George Potter, Philadelphia; John Price, Philadelphia; Voorhees Hogeland, Southampton; J.A. Sanders, Philadelphia; E.M. Brehm, Southampton.

Charles Scott, Southampton; Mrs. William Sinkler, Southampton; Mrs. Arthur Heaton, Southampton; Mrs. Morris Van Hart, Southampton.

The injured all at Abington hospital were: James B. Truitt, Philadelphia, internal injuries; Mrs. Herbert Krusen, Newtown, mother of dead boy, condition far; [illegible], Olney, engineer of No. 151, condition fair; Miss Helen Rook, Newtown, engineer of No. 156, broken

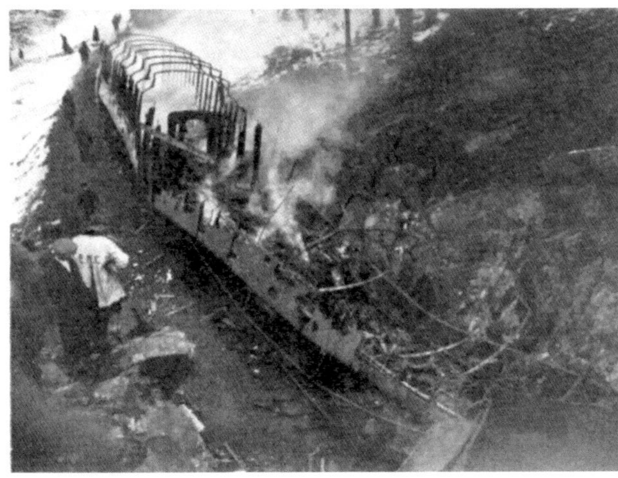

Actual photograph of the aftermath of the train accident that killed twenty-seven people; many were residents of Bucks County. *Upper Southampton Township Historical Advisory Board.*

leg and scalds, serious; William Bixler, Philadelphia, cuts bruises; Miss E. M. Hartman, Ivy Lane, internal injuries, serious; Harold Schneeweis, Churchville, burns and internal injuries, critical condition; Miss Anna Fitzpatrick, Southampton, serious.

Ten others not so seriously hurt were taken to their homes.

Of the twenty-seven who died, eighteen were identified. The unidentified were so burned that officials were unable to match by name, only by those who were reported missing by their loved ones. The nine who were left nameless were buried in a sack cloth together at the cemetery in the back of the North and Southampton Reformed Church on Bristol Road. The memorial headstone dedicated to the victims "in the Bryn Athyn Train Wreck," reads, "That they might have life and that they might have it more abundantly."

PART VIII

Doan Outlaws: The Plumstead Cowboys

The story of the Doans is both romantic and tragic. They were the Sons of respectable Quaker parents, of Plumstead, and during the war, became celebrated for their evil deeds. These five brothers were men of remarkable physical development, tall strong, athletic, and all fine horsemen. Before the war they were men of good reputation, and it is said proposed to remain neutral. Living in a Scotch-Irish settlement, faithful to a man to the cause of Independence, the young Doans were not allowed to take a middle course, and soon they espoused the cause of the crown, which engendered a bitter feeling between them and their Whig neighbors.
—William W.H. Davis

One of the most infamous legends in Bucks County revolves around the Doan Gang, also known as the Doan Outlaws and the Plumstead Cowboys, a notorious gang of Quaker brothers who were most known for robberies and acting as British spies during the American Revolution. According to legend, the gang grew from William Penn's "holy experiment" to establish a community for the Quakers and other religious minorities in what would become Pennsylvania in order to demonstrate their ability to function on their own without persecution. The experiment ultimately failed due to the conflicts between Quakers and non-Quakers over the foundation of Pennsylvania's militia. Bucks County was primarily made up of Quakers who did not support the forthcoming battle with Britain. As a result of William Penn's effort to establish a nation of nations, nearly half of Pennsylvania residents were non-English. Despite Bucks County's overwhelming dislike for the British Crown's actions in the state, the people were more likely to express their concerns through resolutions than violent protests.

The Doan Gang members were Loyalists from a Quaker family of relatively good standing in Plumstead, Bucks County. When the boys were old enough, about the time of the American Revolutionary War, they realized their life careers: killing, stealing and treachery. Three of the Doan members met tragic ends. Moses, who was shot and killed in an attack, was buried in an unmarked grave in Fisherville. Levi and Abraham were buried behind the Plumstead Friends Meeting House, protected by a fieldstone wall that runs along the perimeter. (It is important to note that a Quaker who fought for the Continental Army during the American Revolution would sometimes be buried along the graveyard perimeter.) Their graves bear no inscriptions following the Quaker practice; however, newer headstones were placed to identify them as the infamous outlaws.

To the Doans' family and supporters, the gang was often thought of as Revolutionary-era Robin Hoods who covered areas from Easton to Baltimore and Lancaster to Long Island to steal from the wealthy. Unlike Robin Hood, the outlaws never shared their spoils with the poor or non-elite, yet they were not ruthless outlaws, sometimes expressing moments of humility and a sense of humor up until their capacity for violence grew too large for them to handle.

36

THE DOAN GANG IN BUCKS COUNTY

In 1696, the first of the Doan family moved to Bucks County from Sandwich, Massachusetts, after initially settling throughout Cape Cod in 1629. Others moved to New Jersey and became prominent figures in their communities. Prior to 1726, Israel Doan, father of Joseph Doan Sr., squatted on Native American land in Plumstead Township. The Native Americans would attend monthly Quaker meetings, sometimes carrying weapons on their way in the event they encountered a bear or coyote.

Joseph Doan Sr., father of the outlaws, and his wife, Hester, both prosperous and respected farmers, lived on a farm in a Scots-Irish community along Route 611 south of Plumsteadville. Fathering five of the six Doan outlaws—Joseph Jr., Moses, Aaron, Levi and Mahlon—Joseph Sr. often quarreled with Moses, perhaps sparking the hatred in his son's young heart. The sixth member, Abraham, was their first cousin. These six men would become known as the Doan Gang. As the war approached, the rebels began pressuring those who attempted to remove themselves from the conflict, and with Joseph Sr. being a Quaker, he refused to support either side, marking him as a Loyalist. This caused his farm and property to be raided frequently, and perhaps unfairly, as a large percentage of the county's population had similar beliefs to Joseph's: animals and crops were stolen, property was damaged and Joseph's sons would soon decide it was time to avenge these wrongs.

In 1770, Moses often fought with his father over what some say were trivial matters. Out of stubbornness, Moses refused to settle his woes with his father and fled his home. Several days later, he saved the family of a woman he had loved from an attack by Native Americans, but subsequently, his love for her was declined. Of course, there is no way of knowing that these events set Moses off on his path to crime and notoriety, but it can be speculated that they played a part. Moses's immediate response to his pain and heartbreak was to join a band of Indians from a local tribe and, after expressing his resentment toward the settlers who had been forcing them out, asked to fight alongside the tribe in support of their cause. Unfortunately, there is no known evidence that he joined forces with the Native Americans in an attack on the settlers, but he did, according to family records, develop a "devilish look," letting his hair grow past his shoulders. The following mention of him in history records states that it was soon thereafter that he organized his brothers and set off on their first raid.

A handwritten note written by a great-granddaughter of Joseph Doan, Etta Holloway, tells the story of the outlaws in a manner that seems in support of their actions:

> *They were all of the Quaker faith and did not believe in war. The new government levied a tax upon Joseph, Sr., the father of the Tory Doan boys, confiscated his farm, threw his wife, 3 daughters and youngest son off of the land, jailed Joseph Sr. for non payment of taxes and branded him on his hand as a criminal. This was the given reason for the start of the notorious group known as the Tory Doans.*

Despite her claims, the Pennsylvania Archives date the forfeiture of the Doan's family home as August 13, 1782, ten months after the Doan Gang's robbery of the treasury in Newtown, Bucks County, and after the conclusion of the war.

In the summer of 1776, Moses and Levi met with British general William Howe, offering themselves as spies in support of the Crown. Just one month later, Moses informed Howe of the unprotected Jamaica Pass, which helped Howe defeat General George Washington at the Battle of Long Island on August 27, 1776. Within just a few months, Moses earned a nickname from Major John Andrew, director of British Intelligence Service under Howe: Eagle Spy. Throughout the duration of the first half of the war, the outlaws stole over two hundred horses from Bucks County residents that they would later sell to the Redcoats in Philadelphia.

During General Washington's crossing of the Delaware, it is said that Moses Doan delivered a note to Colonel Rahl's headquarters, stating that Washington and his men would soon be crossing the river to attack. According to the same report, there was a note found in Rahl's vest pocket when his body was recovered at the battle site, stating, "Washington is coming on you down the river, he will be here afore long. [signed] Doan," leaving many to believe that Rahl never read the note, keeping the attack a surprise and handing the extraordinarily pivotal win of the Battle of Trenton to the Continental Army.

In June 1778, Joseph Doan Sr. was listed as a traitor and again relisted in November 1783 alongside over two hundred other men. His sons Aaron, Mahlon and Moses were listed as the same on June 30, 1778.

Soon after providing their assistance to the British army, the Doan Gang, led by Moses, raided nearby rebel farms and banks, sharing their loot with others who experienced the same pain as their family. Despite the Doans having a price on their heads, the rebels were unable to capture the gang through their use of caves as hideouts and supportive neighbors. However, as they continued to rob banks, including the county treasury at Newtown, the Doans quickly lost their community's support and became wanted outlaws. They began their criminal career by plundering and robbing surrounding neighborhoods and homes of local tax collectors and commissioners, including John Thompson of Northampton, soon extending their field of operations to neighboring counties. In 1780, Abraham reportedly raided a home in the extended area, killing a woman in the presence of her nine children. Her husband refuted the report, though it is documented in several sources.

In the fall of 1781, John Hart, a prominent figure in Bucks County, then treasurer, lived in a house in the lower part of Newtown. In the early evening, Moses rode into the town and had Hart's house surrounded, making the man a prisoner. With sentinels keeping watch outside, other members of the gang pillaged the house, obtaining the keys to the treasurer's office. The gang took the opportunity to mock Hart, dressing in his hat, jacket and carrying his lantern to the office. During the robbery of the county treasury, the Doan Gang made off with all of the public money that could be found: £1,307 sterling. Following the raid, the gang met at the Wrightstown schoolhouse and divided their stolen goods.

The following year, the Doans were reported to have robbed nine tax collectors, including several in their homes, in June 1783. A £100 reward was offered for their capture. In July of that same year, Moses, Abraham, Levi, Mahlon and several others robbed four local citizens in their homes, reissuing the reward. During this time, Joseph Jr. attempted to rob Colonel

Robinson's tavern in Dublin, Bucks County, and was shot and captured. He was transported to Philadelphia and imprisoned.

On August 28, 1783, the Doan Gang approached the home of Nathan Halsey in Plumstead Township, requesting food. Halsey sent his son to obtain flour from a nearby mill in Lumberton, New Jersey. The miller objected to his request immediately, but the boy insisted, expressing his concerns for the hungry Doans, whom he reportedly said were at his house. The miller then ground the flour, sent it away with the boy and went to a nearby public sale to inform the townspeople of the Doans' location. A party of approximately fourteen armed men soon dispersed from the sale and armed themselves, taking off to Halsey's. Rumor has it that Colonel Hart was drinking at the Gardenville Tavern, a restaurant that is still in operation today, prior to joining the party and bringing along seven additional men. The men were to meet at a time and place near the house at Cabin Run, where a small stream passes into the west side of Tohickon Creek. With the party dispersing into small groups, they were able to surround the house at a distance and close in on the property as they advanced to prevent escape. Major William Kennedy, Colonel William Hart and Samuel Hart approached the door first. William could reportedly see between the cabin's logs when he approached the house and saw the Doan brothers sitting on a bench eating beans near the fire. Between Samuel and Major Kennedy, William entered the house and ordered for their surrender. The Doans immediately rose from their seats and began firing at them. According to William W.H. Davis, Colonel Hart wrestled Moses to the ground and subdued him. Two other brothers, Abraham and Levi, ran up a ladder and escaped through a small window. The charge of one of the guns cut through the barrel of a gun and lodged itself into Major Kennedy's back, mortally wounding him. Captain Robert Gibson of Fisherville, an area that was once part of Plumstead but would become Plumsteadville, ran into the house and placed his gun to Moses's chest while Hart was holding him to the floor, shooting him through the heart. According to later reports, none of the remaining party members had arrived at the house until the danger was over, leading to the escape of Abraham and Levi. Consequently, for harboring the outlaws, Nathan Halsey was brought to trial, convicted and sentenced to six months' imprisonment. This same day, a note was found on Moses's body threatening the murder of the speaker of the house and Patriot Mulenberg if his brother Joseph was not released from prison. Major Kennedy's funeral would attract the largest crowd in the area, with hundreds of local and state units who visited to pay respects. Kennedy was

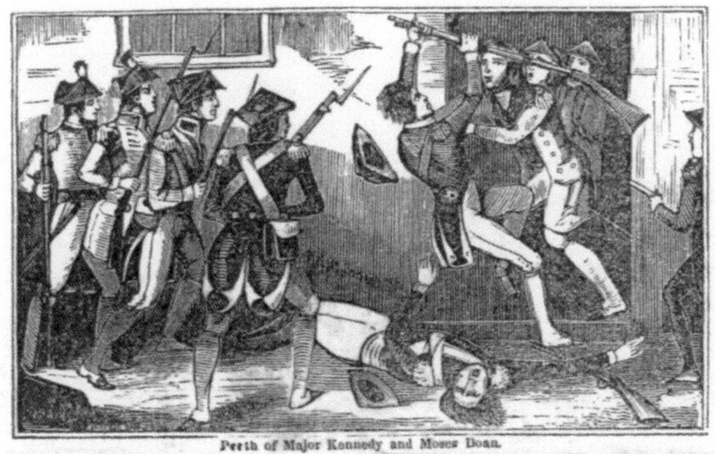

Drawing depicting the deaths of Moses Doan and Major Kennedy at the home of Nathan Halsey, Plumstead Township, Bucks County. August 28, 1783. *Peter Mulcahy.*

buried at the Presbyterian church in Deep Run with full military honors. Legend has it that local man Philip Hinkle dragged Moses's body from the Halsey home to the Doan family homestead in Plumsteadville, dumping the body at the Doan parents' feet, exclaiming, "Here is one of your Tory sons, he won't bother any of us soon again." His body was placed in an unmarked grave that has never been found.

> *Whereas, By depositions taken according to law, it appears that in the night of the twenty-first instant, present month, the dwelling houses of William Darroch, Collector of Taxes, Robert Darroch, Collector of Militia Fines, John Shaw, Robert Gibson, Joseph Greer, and Robert Robinson, in the county of Bucks, within this state, have been broken open, and the said William Darroch, Robert Darroch, John Shaw, Robert Gibson, Joseph Greer and Robert Robinson, robbed of sums of money, and many valuable affects, by Moses Doan, Abraham Doan, Levi Doan, Malin Doan, and other persons unknown.*
>
> —Proclamation, *July 26, 1783*

On September 14, 1783, at the hands of the Pennsylvania legislature, the reward for the remaining outlaws was increased to £300 per outlaw dead, or £100 alive. The Doans were "robbers, felons, burglars, and traitors to the American cause." Additionally, the family of any citizen killed in an attempt to capture one of the outlaws would receive £800. Nearly a month later, Mahlon was arrested in Baltimore, Maryland, for stealing horses and escaped his jail cell by gruesomely cutting off parts of his heels to slip the iron shackles off his ankles. Some reports claim that he drowned while crossing the Chesapeake, but the son of Aaron Doan claimed that Mahlon ran to New York, where he joined other Loyalists and set sail for England. In May 1787, Abraham and Levi were arrested in Chester County and surrendered without a struggle. On September 24, the two brothers were hanged following several attempts at escape. However, the 1785 Treaty of Peace protected them from punishment for their actions during the war, leaving many to believe that their execution served an injustice in light of the treaty. One of their most infamous attempts at escape included their sister, Mary, who baked a saw into a loaf of bread. When that attempt failed, Mary returned, dressed as an elderly Quaker woman visiting all of the imprisoned men. The two cousins were hanged before they were able to saw through the cell bars. Mary repeatedly asked the local Friends meeting to allow their bodies to be buried in the cemetery. Despite the refusal, their graves can be found outside of the back left wall of the cemetery along Ferry Road. In 1784, Joseph Jr. escaped from a jail in Newtown and fled the area. He then changed his name and posed as a teacher in New Jersey for a year before his true identity was uncovered, forcing him to flee to Canada. Aaron Doan was sentenced to hang for outlawry, which was pardoned on the condition that he leave America immediately upon release.

The outlaws were a murderous band of men who stole an incredible amount of money and goods during the American Revolutionary War period and beyond. Legend has it that they buried upward of $100,000 in a wooded area near the Tohickon Creek in Ralph Stover Park in Pipersville, Bucks County. A cave on the park's property is the last known hideout of the Doan Gang. Some say the gold coins are still yet to be found.

The Doans of Bucks County, near Doylestown were also the terror of their day. They were quite as famous in their section of country, and about the Philadelphia lines, as any hero of the revolution. Their father was a man of good estate, and he and his children of good reputation. When the war came on, they proposed to remain neutral; but because of their non-attendance on militia draughts, and refusing to pay fines, they had their property sold occasionally, and themselves harassed. They got inflamed with their neighbours and the revolutionary rulers, and as they found themselves subjected to legal imposts and penalties, five brothers of them set out to live in highways and hedges, and to wage a predatory and retaliatory war upon their persecutors. They were men of fine figures and address—elegant horsemen—great runners, leapers, and excellent at stratagems and escapes. They were true counterparts of Captain Fitz. They delighted to injure public property; but did no injury to the weak, the poor, or the peaceful. They were in league with the British while in Philadelphia, and acted as occasional spies.

—Watson's Annals of Philadelphia and Pennsylvania

PART IX

Historic Cemeteries and Mass Graves in Bucks County

For Revolutionary War soldiers, mass or unmarked graves were the norm. Despite fighting for the country, thousands of soldiers were placed in these graves because there were simply too many bodies. It was near impossible to bury each separately, sometimes because the British troops ordered it, and sometimes to prevent the spread of disease to the living. For other wars, including the Civil War and Spanish-American War, mass graves would occasionally serve as temporary graves until the bodies were transported to their final resting places. Throughout Bucks County and areas across the country, mass graves during the American Revolutionary War became commonplace—some locations are still unknown to this day.

37

PEMBERTON GRAVEYARD AND WATSON GRAVEYARD

Pemberton Graveyard, located in Falls Township, sits near the bank of the Delaware and contains fewer than twenty marked graves—many of the tombstones remain illegible. Two pieces of slate less than an inch in thickness are marked "P.P." and "Phe. P."—both placed close together and assumingly belong to Phineas Pemberton and his wife, Phoebe. Some speculate that the remaining unmarked or illegible graves contain the bodies of various Pemberton family members. Another nearby cemetery, the Watson Graveyard, along the road from Langhorne to Tullytown, is a little less than a half of an acre and is surrounded by a stone wall. The Watson Graveyard was named for a local family who were relatively large land owners during the nineteenth century. Many graves are missing tombstones or were left unmarked. On the same road sits another unmarked cemetery that, unfortunately, has a road running right through it. This one, however, is noted to have contained the bodies of numerous slaves from the area.

38

LANGHORNE BOROUGH UNMARKED CEMETERY

Langhorne grew out of the eighteenth century village of Four Lanes End and this intersection still retains eighteenth century buildings on all four corners with the Richardson House as the oldest documented and best preserved structure.…The house served primarily as the residence of members of the Richardson family from 1738 through the early twentieth century when it was donated for community use to the Langhorne Community Memorial Association.
—National Register of Historic Places Inventory—Nomination Form, United States Department of the Interior, National Park Service

In the early to mid-eighteenth century, Joseph Richardson of present-day Langhorne, Bucks County, then called Attleboro, operated a small store in the west end of a hipped-roof brick and stone house until 1738. Shortly thereafter, he constructed the stone house on the southwest corner, currently still standing, where he opened up shop in the southeast section of the house. The goods sold at his store were brought by boat to Bristol Township and then transported to Attleboro. Before Richardson died in 1772, he exclaimed to a friend: "Thee does not say what thee thinks about it," and in return, his friend responded, "all I have to say is, take care thee does not get to the bottom of thy purse, before thee gets to the top of thy house." It was known that the house was rather costly and elegant.

On the southeast corner sat a house built by Gilbert Hicks, who would later sell it along with forty acres of land to William Goforth. During the American Revolutionary War, the house was used as a hospital to treat

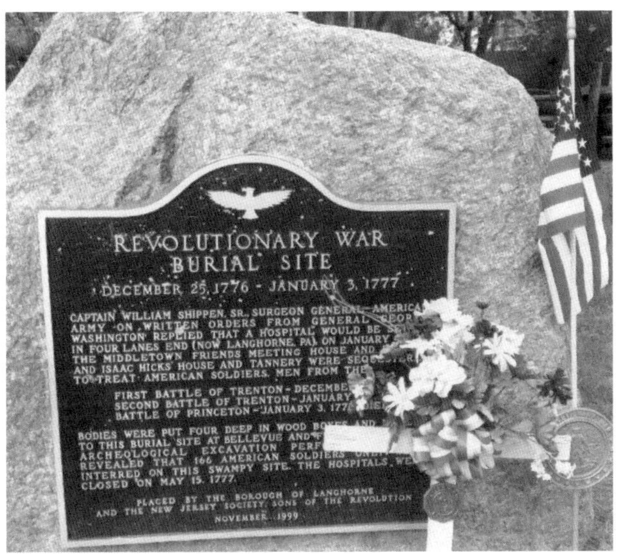

Monument dedicated to Continental Army soldiers from the Revolutionary War buried in mass grave, Langhorne, Bucks County.

wounded and dying Continental Army soldiers. General Washington's soldiers occupied four dwellings in the town following the Battle of Trenton: the Middletown Monthly Meeting and its school, the Isaac Hicks House and Hicks' tannery. These four buildings were most likely the only military hospitals north of Philadelphia. Records indicate that approximately 166 soldiers from the winter campaign of 1776 were buried in a nearby open lot. Many of these soldiers did not die of wounds in battle but rather from starvation, disease and illness. Joseph Richardson's eleven-year-old daughter, Jane, witnessed the burial of the soldiers in that graveyard. In the journal of Joshua Richardson II, Jane described what she witnessed from the window of her house. Watching sleds with coffins being pulled to the burial site, Jane saw three to four soldiers placed in shallow graves numerous times for the next five months. According to some reports, the winter ground was so frozen the bodies were placed in shallow graves on the property as the mourners were unable to dig any deeper. When spring arrived, the odor was so strong the grave was immediately filled with dirt. A memorial and informative plaque sits at the site of the mass grave.

In 1992, evidence gathered through a request to verify the journal's legitimacy confirmed the burial site by finding rose-head coffin nails with wood fragments still attached.

CROSS KEYS CEMETERY

Cross Keys Cemetery, located in Plumstead Township near present-day Pine Run Road and Old Dublin Pike, is a historic graveyard containing the remains of over forty locals beginning in the mid-eighteenth century. The burial ground sat in the corner of the fifty-plus-acre property of Christopher Day, one of Bucks County's first residents, who reportedly settled in Plumstead Township in the late seventeenth century. His son, Christopher Day II, was born in the township in the year 1680. Day donated the land for the first cemetery and school in the township. According to William W.H. Davis's history on the graveyard, at the time of his writing in 1876, the property was nearly in ruins, with only forty gravestones still standing. Christopher Day wrote in his will on September 1, 1746, that he intended "ten perches square for a graveyard forever." Day was the first to be buried on the property; his son followed nearly fifteen years later. Two stones were in memory of Abraham Fried, died December 21, 1772, at thirty-two years old; and William Daves, February 22, 1815, sixty-eight. According to W.W.H. Davis, Fried and Daves, "a black man," were memorialized with the most "pretentious" stones made of marble. It is likely that the early Welsh Baptists of New Britain buried their deceased in the cemetery until they established their own church. Legend has it that a previous owner of the property removed all the stones during the late twentieth century because she feared vandals and thieves. The majority of the tombstones were lost to history.

Washington Crossing
Unknown Graves

The Thompson-Neely House, located on part of the land managed by Washington Crossing Historic Park, or the "Upper Park," served as a temporary army hospital during General Washington's famous winter campaign of 1776–77 and the Battle of Trenton. Many ill and wounded soldiers were carried to the homestead owned by the Thompson and Neely families, including James Monroe, who would later become the fifth president of the United States, wounded during the First Battle of Trenton as an officer, as well as General Washington's cousin William who was also injured during the campaign and subsequently treated at the homestead. On Christmas Day, 1776, twenty-four-year-old Captain James

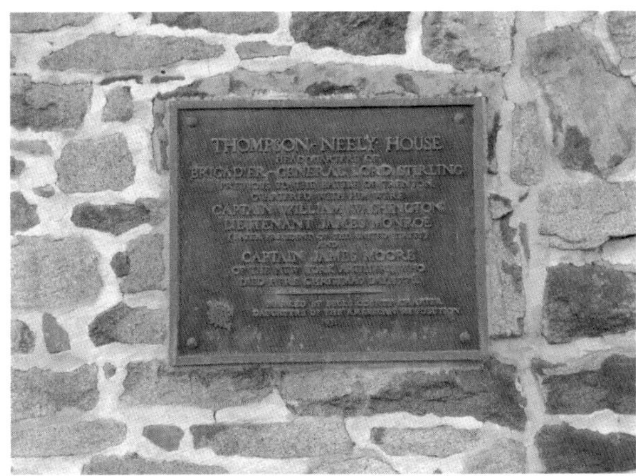

Thompson-Neely House marker, stating that homestead was headquarters of Brigadier General Lord Stirling, quartered with Captain William Washington, Lieutenant James Monroe and Captain James Moore. New Hope, Bucks County.

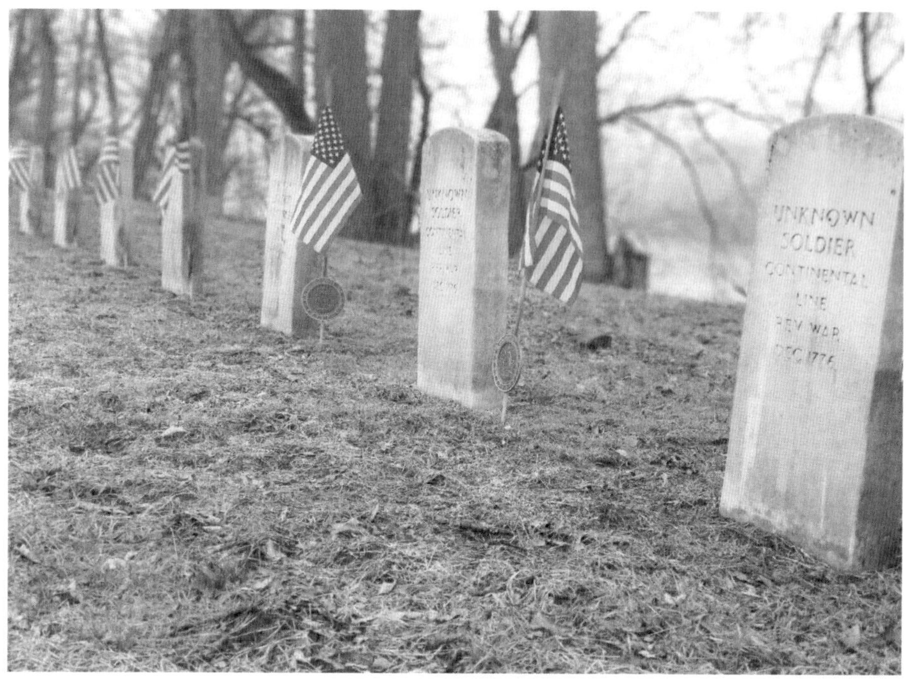

Image of soldiers' graves, Washington Crossing Upper Park. In proximity to the Thompson-Neely House.

Moore of Alexander Hamilton's New York Artillery died of camp fever and was buried on the property alongside other men who died during the campaign. Moore's is the only identified grave. The cemetery is a short five-minute walk from the Thompson-Neely House. Despite there being several standing memorial stones, the number of Continental soldiers buried there is unknown. Many American soldiers died of illness, disease or previous injuries—none were known to have been killed during the First Battle of Trenton and Washington's crossing of the Delaware. Captain Moore's original memorial, which was replaced several years ago, was inscribed, "To the memory of Cap. James Moore of the New York Artillery; Son of Benjamin & Cornelia Moore of New York; He died Decm. The 25th A.D. 1776 Aged 24 Years & Eight Months."

SLATE HILL CEMETERY

Slate Hill Cemetery, located in Lower Makefield, Bucks County, was established in 1690 and is often thought to be the oldest burial ground in Bucks County. There are numerous unmarked graves for which the dates are unknown to this day. The headstones are said to mark the graves of a number of Lower Makefield's first settlers. The cemetery was created in three sections: a tract granted by Thomas Janney in 1690, by Abel Janney in 1721 northwest alongside Yardley-Morrisville Road and the final section granted by Joshua Anderson in 1788 to expand even further.

Many of the graves are from the early eighteenth century, representing Bucks County's first settlers. The Quaker Friends section contains over four hundred graves, with fewer than two hundred marked. Most of the burials occurred prior to the nineteenth century according to a 1941 survey sponsored by the Pennsylvania Historical Commission. Within the Friends area, over 80 percent of markers are made of brownstone, while approximately two dozen are made of wood or wire wickets. This same section of the cemetery contains the only known seventeenth-century gravestone in Bucks County, dated 1698. The last known person to have been buried in the cemetery is Martha E. White, in 1918. Containing the graves of six free African Americans who served in the Civil War, Slate Hill Cemetery remains one of the most significant burial grounds in Bucks County.

BUCKINGHAM FRIENDS MEETING CEMETERY

The Buckingham Friends Cemetery, which sits directly behind the Buckingham Friends Meeting House in Lahaska, Bucks County, has been in operation for over three centuries, since 1705, even before the first meetinghouse was constructed. The cemetery was surrounded by stone walls, except for its north side, in 1752, and in 1805, the burial ground was extended farther north. During the Revolutionary War, the Buckingham Friends Meeting House was activated as an army hospital for wounded, ill and dying soldiers of the Continental Army. These soldiers were buried on the meetinghouse's property, either in the graveyard or just outside. There also was an area of the cemetery dedicated to the burial of African Americans during the nineteenth century. Reportedly, there are several Native American graves located in the cemetery.

Despite the cemetery officially opening in 1705, the earliest remaining gravestones are dated in the late eighteenth century, as Quakers did not commonly mark their deceased with headstones until about 1790. In 1706, the Buckingham Meeting House noted that "it is altogether wrong and of evil tendency for to have any grave stones or any other sort of monument over or about the graves." As of today, there are over 2,500 headstones; however, several have either sunk in the ground, tilted from heavy snows and harsh weather or completely fallen or crumbled.

In 2011, the cemetery underwent a massive restoration project to remove rotted shingles and anchors and repair the dilapidated stone walls. Keeping as much of the original concrete as possible, anchors were cut according

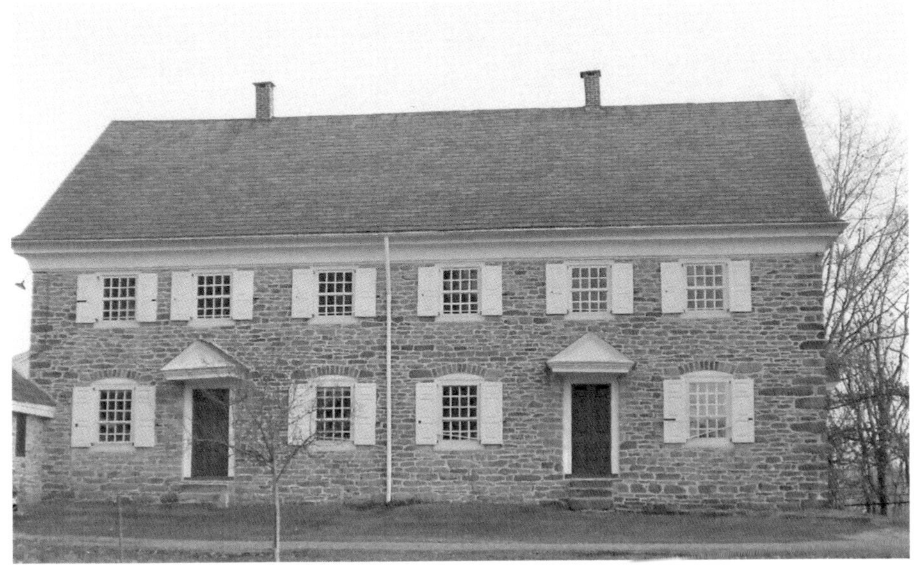

Buckingham Friends Meeting House, Buckingham, Bucks County. Built 1768. The first meetinghouse on the site was constructed of logs in 1705 by English Quakers.

to size, nailed together and then cemented in place. Cypress boards were positioned on each side, and a trim board was nailed along the bottom edge. The anchors and shingles were cut weeks prior, and all of the work completed was done so through the tremendous work of volunteers.

The Buckingham Meeting House was designated as a National Historic Landmark in 2003. Within the walls, there are various unmarked (and an unknown number of) African American graves from the time of the Underground Railroad, as well as the aforementioned Revolutionary War soldiers.

43

Warminster Township Mass Graves

The locations of two mass gravesites in Warminster of Continental militia killed at the Battle of Crooked Billet on May 1, 1778, remained a mystery for many years. In the township's 275-year anniversary booklet, the location of one graveyard was recorded by the township's historian Paul Bailey. This mass cemetery is located at the Noble Family Graveyard near the intersection of County Line Road and Madison Avenue in Warminster. According to William W.H. Davis, the other mass gravesite, located near what is now Warminster Heights, was unknown for numerous years. Steve Kluskiewicz, company surveyor of the township's contracted engineering company Gilmore and Associates, used the approximate location of the Noble graveyard and was able to update the original recordings with GPS to produce an approximate location. Currently, there is no marker indicating where this mass grave is in the township. There is, however, a historic marker on the lawn of Tri-County Electric Company on Jacksonville Road that was installed in 1928, indicating two mass gravesites.

UPPER SOUTHAMPTON OLD SCHOOL MEETING HOUSE

Located at the intersection of Second Street Pike and Maple Avenue in Upper Southampton Township sits the Old School Meeting House, also commonly known as the Old School Baptist Church. The Southampton Old School Baptist Church, built in 1773 and expanded in 1814, is the oldest of its kind in Bucks County. John Hart, a Quaker freeholder from Oxfordshire, England, had purchased one thousand acres from William Penn on the Poquessing Creek near Byberry and Warminster in 1682. Hart was committed to his political and religious life in Philadelphia and was elected to the first Pennsylvania assembly, voting in approval of the first charter of government. Hart, clerk of the Philadelphia Quaker Meeting House, was often thought of as a man of rank and character and a good preacher. On his Byberry farm, Hart set up a burial plot, first used in 1683, and within four years, he held regular Quaker meetings of worship in his home.

The church traces its roots back to a dispute in 1691 between the Society of Friends and local prominent Quaker George Keith. The dispute, which began when Keith favored the idea that the Friends should adopt a profession of faith, led to his followers to be known as "Keithians." One group of Keithians met in Southampton and was eventually permitted to join in worship with the Lower Dublin Baptist Church in 1702. In 1731, an area resident gifted the Keithians with an acre of land at the intersection of Maple Road and Second Street Pike, as well as over one hundred acres to support the ministry. It was then that a log church was constructed alongside a small

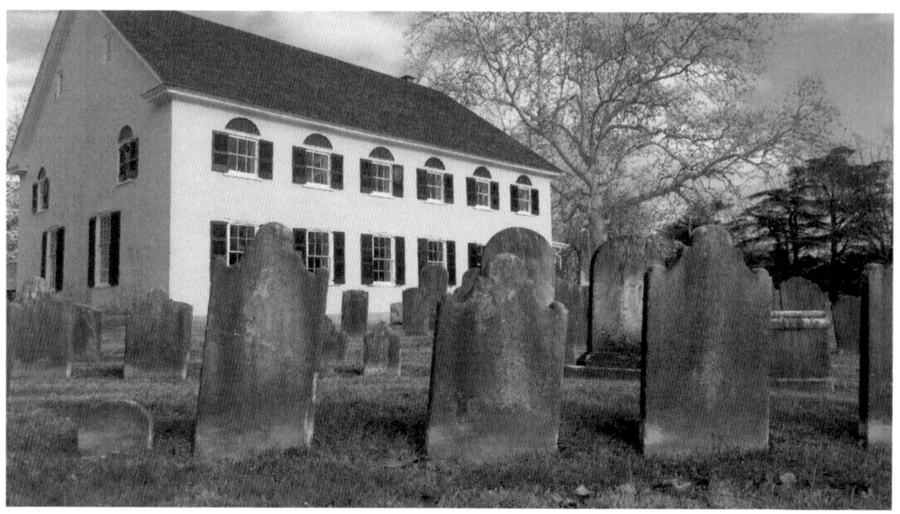

The Southampton Old School Baptist Church. Built in 1773, enlarged in 1814. Upper Southampton Township, Bucks County.

stream, which may have been used for baptisms. In 1745, Southampton worshippers petitioned for the severing of ties with the Lower Dublin Baptist Church, which was approved in 1746, leading to the new church covenant for Southampton Baptist Church being signed that same year. Even though George Keith eventually convinced Hart of his ideals, their friendship would not last more than ten years, for the Quaker Yearly Meeting disowned Keith for his views on Quakerism.

Several church followers are classified as Patriots for the roles they played in the American Revolutionary War. Joseph Hart, grandson of John, became a deacon of the meeting and sheriff of Bucks County. Hart played a monumental role in organizing Patriots, later becoming a colonel in General George Washington's army. Hart supplied blankets and provisions for nearly two hundred men at Valley Forge. William VanHorn, a Southampton minister, enlisted in the Continental Army and became a chaplain at Valley Forge. It is said that he rode his horse from Valley Forge to Southampton every Sunday to preach for the congregation. David Jones, another chaplain, served the Continental Army under General Anthony Wayne, tending to hundreds of wounded in battles from Brandywine to Yorktown. Jones was known as a strong-willed, fighting chaplain who was able to boost morale of the soldiers so well that British commander Lord Howe offered a reward for his capture. At the conclusion of the war, Jones became minister in

Southampton for six years. At the age of seventy-six, he enlisted as a chaplain for the War of 1812. Thomas Montanye, also a minister at Southampton, often preached to the American troops who assembled to defend Baltimore.

Six veterans of the French and Indian Wars and twenty-four soldiers of the American Revolution are buried in the cemetery. A descendant of the original Hart family, John, was killed during the Civil War just four days before General Lee's surrender at the Battle of Appomattox Court House. Hart is buried in the cemetery. His headstone lists the battles in which he fought.

History lives here in Bucks County; it is the living, breathing schematic of the lives of every one of us, as well as those who came before us. The struggles and the triumphs, the happiness and the sorrow, are the building blocks on which this county was founded. History was yesterday and last year and a thousand years ago, and it is tomorrow. History forms and shapes how we live and reminds us of how we came to be where we are now. History should be treasured, preserved and remembered for future generations. The events, both momentous and trivial, that occurred here in Bucks County made this county what it is today: a true melting pot of people—descendants of the county's first settlers and those who arrived later. It is both a romantic story and a tragic story, pairing history with untold tales, as well as those that have been remembered. Bucks County's rolling hills and spacious fields meet suburbia, beckoning us to the places we call home. There are many more places to explore here in historic Bucks County, even more influential events to discover and many more tales to tell, uncovering the hidden history of Bucks County.

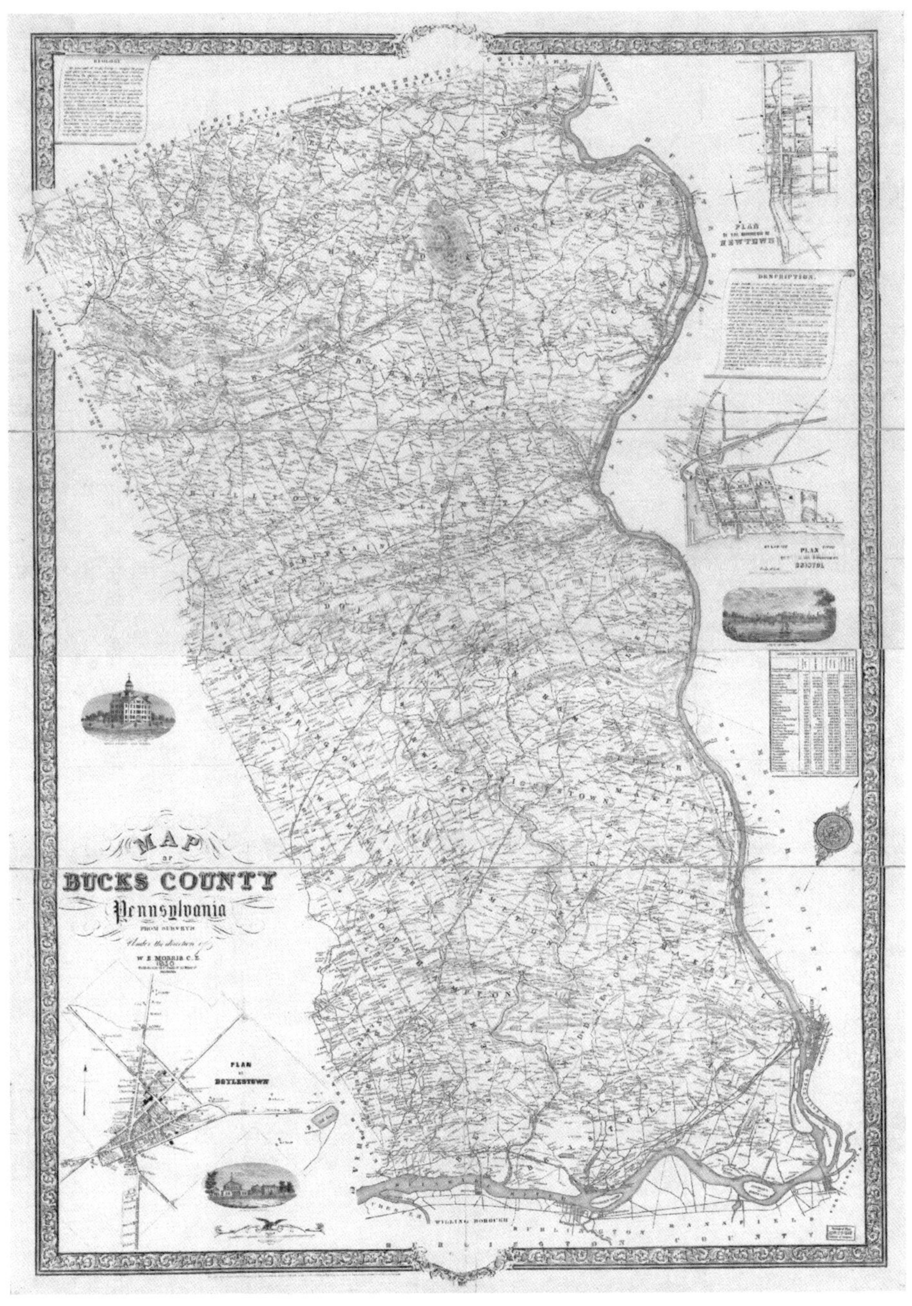

Map of Bucks County, Pennsylvania. 1850. William E Morris, Robert Pearsall Smith. Created/Published by R.P. Smith, Philadelphia, 1850. *Library of Congress, Geography and Map Division.*

BIBLIOGRAPHY

Bailey, Paul C. *A History of Warminster Township, The First 275 Years*. Warminster, PA: Warminster Township 275th Anniversary Commission, 1986.

Davis, William Watts Hart. *The History of Bucks County, Pennsylvania: From the Discovery of the Delaware to the Present Time*. Democrat Book and Job Office Print, 1876. Digitized September 11, 2006.

Doane, Alfred A. *The Doane Family and Their Descendants*. N.p., 1902.

Duess, Marie Murphy. *Colonial Inns and Taverns of Bucks County: How Pubs, Taprooms and Hostelries Made Revolutionary History*. Charleston, SC: The History Press, 2007.

Ely, Warren S., and Harvey K. Crouthamel. *History of the General Greene Inn*. Conducted by Harvey K. Bucks County Historical Society. Ivyland, PA: Ivy Press, 1918.

———. *On the Old York Road, The Ancient Highway from Philadelphia to New York*. Ivyland, PA: Ivy Press, 1918.

Hotchkin, Samuel F. *The Bristol Pike*. Philadelphia: George W. Jacobs, 1893.

Journal of Joseph Lehman Eisenbrey. Mercer Museum. MSC 163. Doylestown, Pennsylvania.

Magill, Edward H. "The Underground Railroad in Bucks County, Pennsylvania." *Friends Intelligencer*, 1898.

Rivinus, William M. *Early Taverns of Bucks County*. New Hope, PA: 1963.

Rogers, John P. *The Doan Outlaws, Or, Bucks County's Cowboys in the Revolution*. Doylestown, PA: Doylestown Publishing Company, 1897.

I have also consulted various Bucks County Township and Historical Society websites and materials while completing research for the book, including the Bucks County Historical Society, Upper Southampton Township, Upper Southampton Historical Advisory Board, Langhorne Historical Association and Solebury Township Historical Society.

INDEX

M

N

O

P

Q

R

About the Author

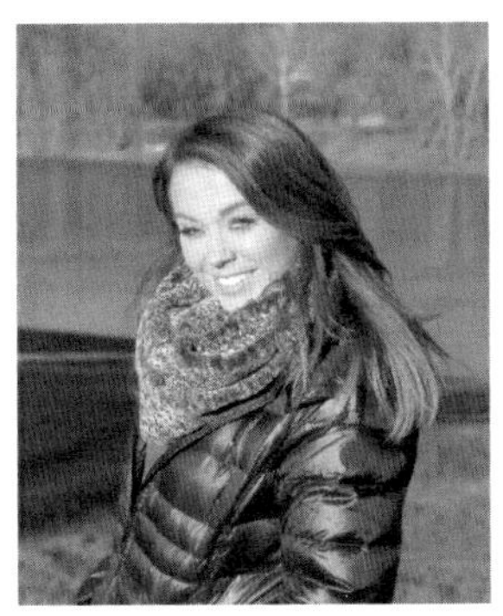

Jennifer Rogers, author. Washington Crossing State Park.

Jennifer Rogers is a passionate historian who dedicates her time to the preservation of local history through her volunteer efforts with several organizations. She was appointed to the Upper Southampton Historical Advisory Board and serves as president of the Craven Hall Historical Society. As a graduate of Pennsylvania State University, Jennifer Rogers obtained her Bachelor of Arts in American Studies with a minor in English. While studying at Penn State, Jennifer interned at the Spruance Library at Mercer Museum, where she discovered and transcribed a Civil War soldier's diary, completed two undergraduate research projects and also presented her research and transcriptions of the Bucks County Civil War soldier's diary at the Pennsylvania Historical Association's Annual Conference. For over two years, she was the collections manager, as well as a preservation and communications associate for the SS *United States Conservancy*, the fastest surviving passenger ocean liner—even larger than the *Titanic*. In 2022, Jennifer received her Master of Science in History & Archaeology from the University of Edinburgh, Scotland, while also serving as a student representative. Over the next few years, Rogers hopes to continue preserving Bucks County's abundant history all while educating surrounding communities of what the county truly has to offer.